GAME DAY MEMORIES

Tailgaters, Touchdowns & Traditions!

Mary Jane Nielsen · Jonathan Roth · Beth Vogel · Russ Vogel

Cover Design by Mary Jane Nielsen, Jon Roth, Beth Vogel and Russ Vogel
Page Design and Layout by Mary Jane Nielsen, Jon Roth, Beth Vogel and Russ Vogel

Unless otherwise specified, the photography used in this book is taken from the Edholm & Blomgren Collection.

Whenever possible we have tried to credit the Nebraska State Historical Society for images from the MacDonald Collection, however, these images also exist in our negative holdings and we reserve the right to use them.

Printed in U.S.A. by Settell's Printing, Lincoln, Nebraska
ISBN 978-0-41028-9

For Mom:
A Game Day isn't a Game Day without your "Go Baby, Go Baby, Go Baby Go!" "Get'em! Get'em!" and "Yipee!"

For Dad:
Your quiet, calm, thoughtful analysis of the game has always taught us something about the game of life.
Mary Jane & Beth

To the greatest Husker fan I know. Win or lose, you're always behind them. I love you for that and so much more.
Jon

For Dad:
Your enthusiasm and zest, not just for Nebraska Football, but for life in general, has made a great impression on your son.
Russ

Game Day Memories would not have been possible without some greatly appreciated help from the following contributors:

Cover Memorabilia
MJN Vision Collection
JMJ Inspirations Collection
Beth & Russ Vogel
Tom Hinds
Brayden & Christian Remington

Memorabilia
MJN Vision
JMJ Inspirations
Mary Jane Nielsen
Jon Roth
Bryan & Heather Martin
Sam & Cheri Thaller
Brayden Remington
Christian Remington
Beth & Russ Vogel
Chad Maun
Jeff Jones
Dan Wagner
John Belz

Photos
Nebraska State Historical Society
University of Nebraska
Edholm & Blomgren
American Red Cross
Lincoln Police Department
Bob & Sharon Hitz

Memories & History Selections from
Midge Alfieri, 126
American Builder Magazine, 14
Bob Ammon, 134
John Belz, 190
Jeff Buss, 150
Pete Debus, 40
In fond memory
of Jerry Delzell, 153
Rick Dolen,169
Joyce Donlan, 115
Evie Dorn, 173
Ron Douglas, 34
Amy Frohn, 184
Wallace Gake, 71
Mr & Mrs. Dwayne
"Goldie" Goldsmith, 69
Fred Hall, 152
Kay & Kep Harding, 176
Herbert G. Henry, 68
Sandy Hergert, 66
Tom Hinds, 128
Mary Jo Iwan, 188
Randall S. Jones, 174
Karen Kammann, 187
Joyce Lattimer, 146
Gwen Lindberg, 116
John Linhardt, 122
Susan McCoy, 154
Jill R. Micek, 158
Frank Mulvey, 39
Mary Jane Nielsen, 192
Vemmy Nielsen, 76, 78
Pat Holle Novak, 189
Deb Oman, 184
Lois Poppe, 130
Lavern Priest, 141
Jon Roth, 40, 167
Gil Savery, 42, 62
Becky Schenaman, 180
Rita Schriner, 173
Jack Schubert, 67
Clark Splichal, 121
Victoria Springer, 191
Tales of the Cornhuskers
Jan Thelen, 188
Charis Thomas & Herbie, 110
Dave Thurber, 170
University of Nebraska
Beth Vogel, 164
Ron Vogel , 52
Russ Vogel, 182
Muffy Vrana, 142
Les Williams, 178
Dwyane Wittstruck, 84
Don Workman, 138

Special Thanks to:
Dick & Sue Blomgren
Cathy Blythe KFOR Radio
Dennis Buckley
The Neighborhood Extra
Settell's Printing
A to Z Printing
NECO Security
Don & Vemmy Nielsen
Bill, Cathy and Charis Thomas
Ron Vogel

Table of Contents

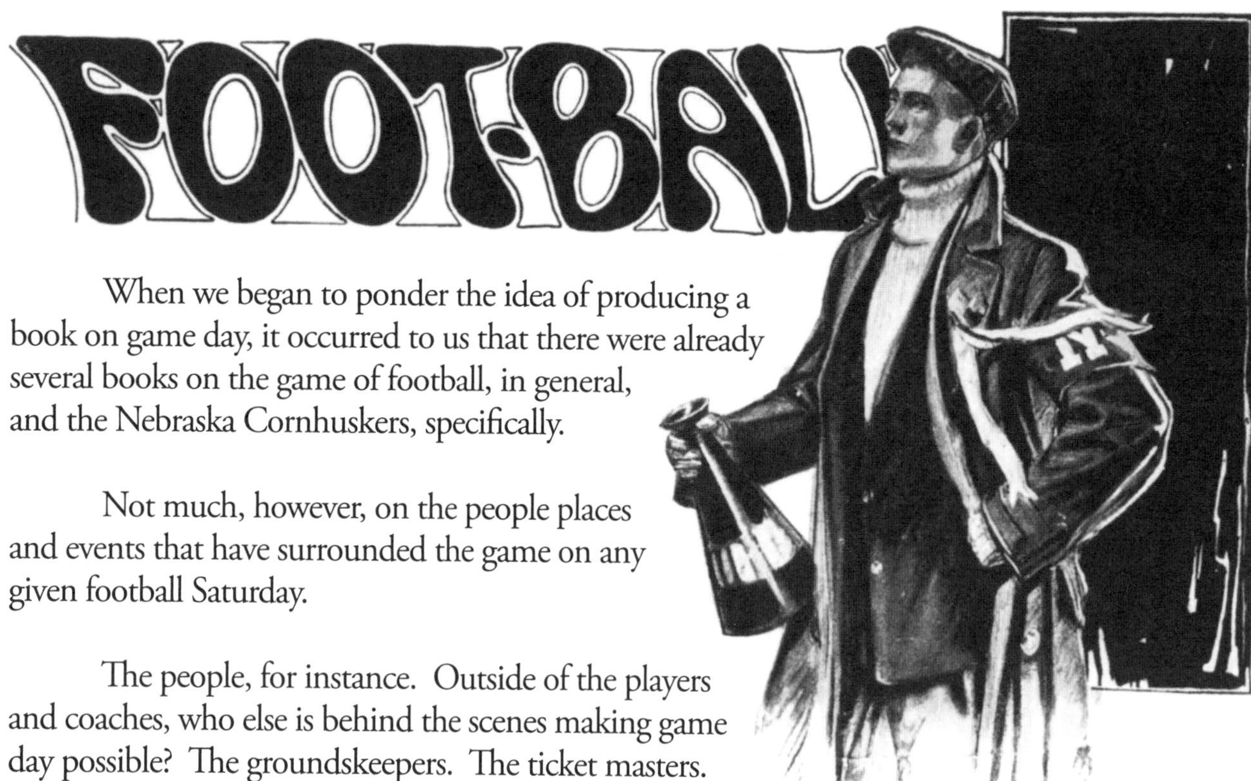

When we began to ponder the idea of producing a book on game day, it occurred to us that there were already several books on the game of football, in general, and the Nebraska Cornhuskers, specifically.

Not much, however, on the people places and events that have surrounded the game on any given football Saturday.

The people, for instance. Outside of the players and coaches, who else is behind the scenes making game day possible? The groundskeepers. The ticket masters. The concessionaires. That youthful usher who was always ready, willing and able to guide you to your personally-selected vantage point of the game.

What of the merchants who did their level best to entice us into their stores by offering a free bus ride to the stadium or perhaps some free parking?

And we can't forget those many retauranteurs and tavern keepers, who by virtue of the fine foods and the ambience they served up, beckoned us into their establishments for a dose of midwest hospitality that always seemed to heighten the game day atmosphere, way before and long after the last balloon had sailed out of Memorial Stadium.

We thank all those who contributed stories, photos and memorabilia that helped bring Game Day Memories to light. When we encounter all the little jewels that jog a memory, we can't help but want to share them with you. Even by university reference standards, finding a yearbook or a piece of memorabilia in good condition becomes more and more challenging as the years pass.

If you have some great form of reference in your possession, please share it with us. Our purpose is, first and foremost, to share with everyone what we have learned from others.

Mary Jane Nielsen, Jonathan Roth, Beth Vogel, Russ Vogel

Chapter One

The Dawn of Game Day

Origin of the Cornhusker Nickname

Before 1900, Nebraska football teams were known by such names as the Old Gold Knights, Antelopes, Rattlesnake Boys and the Bugeaters. In its first two seasons (1890-91), Nebraska competed as the Old Gold Knights, but beginning in 1892, Nebraska adopted Scarlet and Cream as its colors and accepted the Bugeaters as its most popular nickname until the turn of the century. Named after the insect-devouring bull bats that hovered over the plains, the Bugeaters also found their prey in the Midwest, enjoying winning campaigns in every year of the 1890s until a disappointing season in 1899.

After its first losing season in a decade, it must have seemed only fitting that Nebraska move in a new direction, and Lincoln sportswriter Charles S. (Cy) Sherman, who was to gain national renown as the sports editor of the Lincoln Star and help originate The Associated Press Poll, provided the nickname that has gained fame for a century. Sherman tired of referring to the Nebraska teams with such an unglamorous term as Bugeaters. Iowa had, from time to time, been called the Cornhuskers, and the name appealed to Sherman.

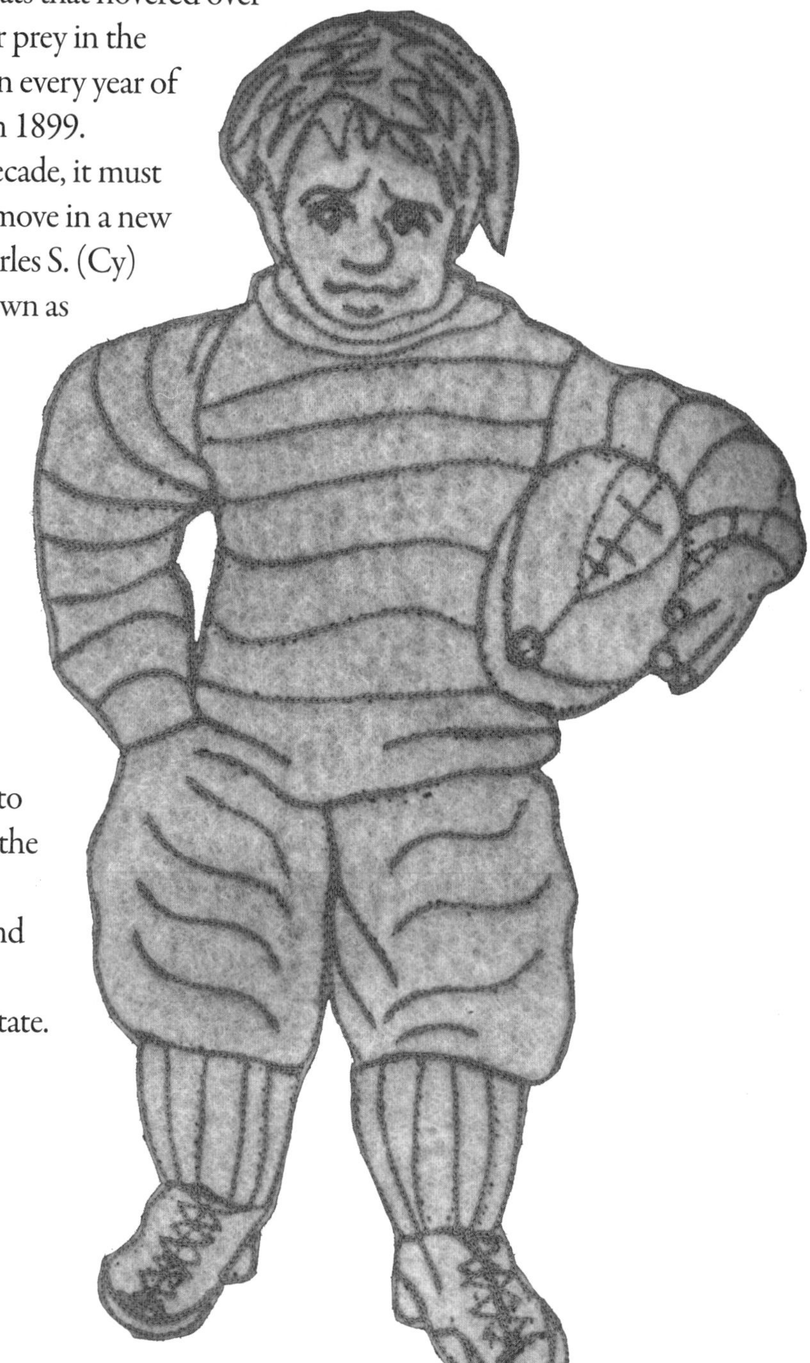

Iowa partisans seemed to prefer Hawkeyes, so Sherman started referring to the Nebraska team as Cornhuskers, and the 1900 team was first to bear that label.

Of course, the name caught on and became a Nebraska byword, eventually becoming the official nickname for the state.

Huskers NSide

Courtesy of University of Nebraska

The Fan

I was one of the thousands who hollered themselves hoarse when the first Scarlet and Cream jersey showed inside the fence... I played no small part... I played a great game–on the bleachers... I had tears in my eyes one moment, and blood the next. I don't think I sat down at all during the whole course of the game and I don't recall having noticed anyone else using that privilege.

Gee, but that was some game.

Every time I close my eyes even now I can see those huge stands waving and trembling under their weight of gaily clad eager humanity...The roar that seemed never to die, as the two teams trotted on the field. The deathly silence, and the bated breath that hung on the whistle just before the first kick-off. The trembling knees, the straining eyes, the tense nerves. The final soul–at last to the ground, and the real game was won.

The Girl's Section The girls section, or rather the idea of having a girls' section, originated in the mind of "Dog" last fall, when he was considering the best method of securing the attendance of the co-ed contingent at football games. It was, you will remember, in the days before Chancellor Avery made his famous exhortation for the "cussless victory," that the girls first had a section of the big stands assigned for their sole use, occupation, and enjoyment. This gave the boys an opportunity to express their opinion of the referee and the opposing players without trammel. It gave the girls the same opportunity of course, but no one would be so rude as to suggest that any availed themselves of it. It also presented new ground for decorative effects, and permitted the female of the species to appear at the game enrobed in all the fur and fine feathers papa could afford. The girls availed themselves of the opportunity, and the college exchanges of the country were unanimous in approving the decoration of the girls' section at Nebraska. We thought something of it ourselves. In years to come the section may wax larger, but in quality there is small room for improvement to the CORNHUSKER'S way of thinking.

Stories and photos taken from 1912 Cornhusker Annual

Game Days of the Bugeaters

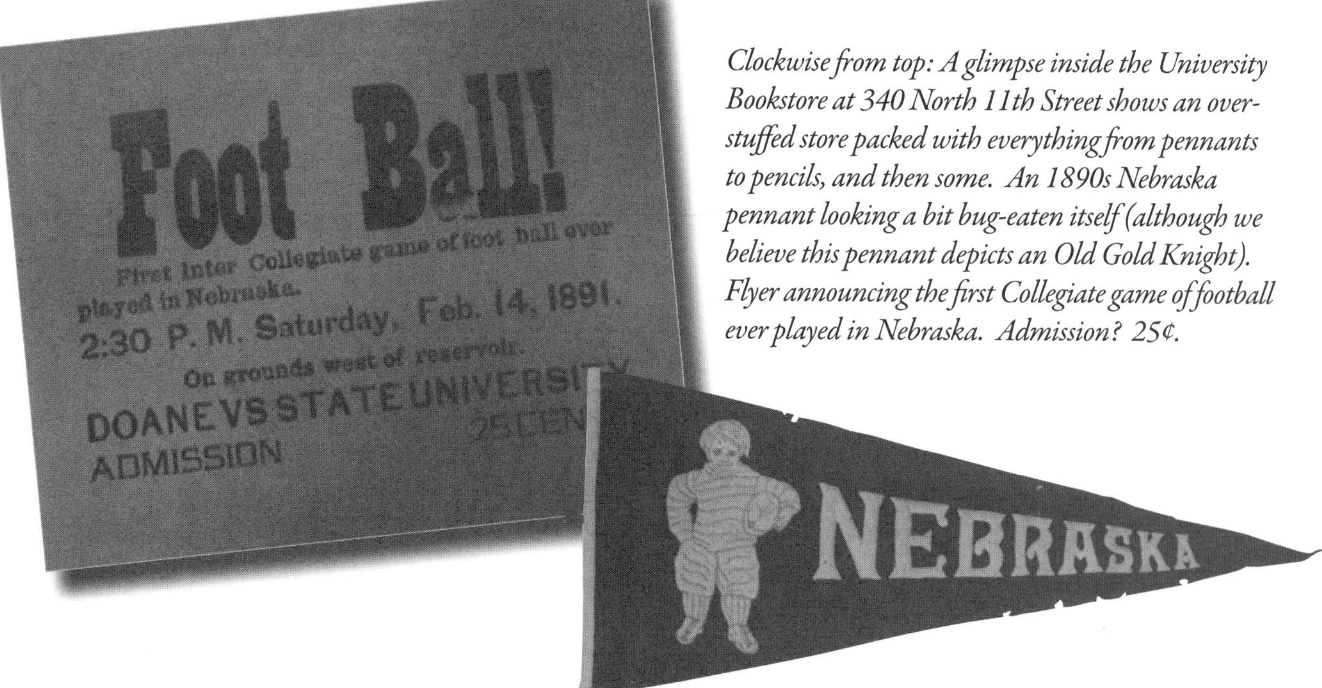
Foot Ball!
First Inter Collegiate game of foot ball ever played in Nebraska.
2:30 P. M. Saturday, Feb. 14, 1891.
On grounds west of reservoir.
DOANE VS STATE UNIVERSITY
ADMISSION 25 CENTS

Clockwise from top: A glimpse inside the University Bookstore at 340 North 11th Street shows an over-stuffed store packed with everything from pennants to pencils, and then some. An 1890s Nebraska pennant looking a bit bug-eaten itself (although we believe this pennant depicts an Old Gold Knight). Flyer announcing the first Collegiate game of football ever played in Nebraska. Admission? 25¢.

IOWA 0. – NEBRASKA 12. 1913.
UNIVERSITY OF NEBRASKA.
NEBRASKA
Shenka tears up the Tigers
Missouri punts from Goal.

Dear Old Nebraska U

University of Nebraska

Words and Music by
HARRY PECHA
Arranged by Wm. T. Quick

Tempo di Valse

There is no place like Ne-bras -

U. ____ Where the girls are the fair-

an- ... that I knew. ____

br... ____ We'll all stick to-

geth-er, In all kinds of weath-er, For dear old Ne-bras -

NEBRASKA

NEBRA

Used with permission of Harry Pecha

University of Nebraska.
Chapter founded 1898.
ROBERT W. STEVENS.
1. Come a run - nin', boys, Don't you hear that noise
2. When the sun is bright And the fields are ripe
Like the thun - der in the sky?
With the tas - sel on the corn,
- bras - ki. Now it's
ly morn. In the
With a cheer That will sweep all foes a - way; So
'Tis the air That in - spires us with a zest, That
(116)
UNIVERSITAS NEBRASKENSIS.
FEB. 15. 1869.
I Am Backing The Team
THE UNIVERSITY OF NEBRASKA
Department of Physical Education and Athletics
1921-22
No.
Student Athletic Ticket
PRICE $10.00 Tax Free
PURCHASER
THIS TICKET IS NON-transferable. The management will not be responsible for lost or mutilated tickets.
No. 48
ATHLETIC EVENT
9
No. 48
ATHLETIC EVENT
8
No. 48
ATHLETIC EVENT
16

The $1,000,000 Memorial Stadium erected at the University of Nebraska, Lincoln. John Latenser & Sons and Davis & Wilson, Associate Architects

Nebraska University Stadium

Setting for Athletic Games Erected of Concrete; to Accommodate 40,000 Persons; Cost, $1,000,000.

In a number of ways the new University Stadium recently completed in Lincoln, Neb., is unique. Any building enterprise of this nature is unique for that matter because the builders and manufacturers involved are not serving a standard job when they tackle a proposition of this sort.

A large sum of money is often involved and sometimes the bidders may wonder if their pay is going to be in the envelope when the time arrives. That is one problem. Another is that the people to be directly pleased are often men of every walk of life-men who formerly sang those college songs and yelled those college yells-but who of late have gone into enterprises so far apart that to present a set of plans that are practical, that come within the means available and to have these plans suit everybody; is nothing much short of a phenomenon.

Nebraska for several years has been recognized as a formidable athletic foe by other like institutions and she has been holder of her own with the best of them. But her football field was almost a disgrace. Flanked on both sides by rickety, wooden seats who underpinning on more than one occasion caused, by giving away under extra weight, about as much excitement as the game itself; only those vitally interested in the contests seem to care to go.

The athletic board realized that to match the local team with hardened warriors of distant states required a tremendous expense, and expense that the old field could not return because the seating capacity was so limited. This realization brought about the first definite movement for a stadium. At once money to pay for the thing was the paramount issue. To swell the ranks of the alumni, all former students, whether graduates or not, were granted a place on the list.

With this host of loyal people, a subscription drive was started and the amounts as they came in were made known through the press by bulletin boards. And in time $700,000 had been pledged.

But what about the plans? We talk of loyalty. We say we would go the limit for the sake of the old school. But how many of us would finance the drawing for all working plans from the preliminary to the finished set and with an elaborate wash drawing thrown in?

To Mr. John Latenser and Mr. Ellery Davis, both former students and graduates, goes the credit in large part for putting over the enterprise. Both men are successful architects. Both men still retain that subtle thing-college spirit and college loyalty. And these men put their heads together and decided to go the limit.

The result was the complete plans drawn to scale, all dimensions of value shown, together with other necessary data logically coming from the designers. After long hours, and days, and weeks of work the plans were given-gratis!

The concrete construction on the underside of the stands. Everything shown above the ground is concrete.

Actual work was commenced May 20, 1923. The concrete work bid was awarded to the Parsons Construction Company of Omaha, Neb., for $456,000. Work in the form of a sub-contract and for a consideration of $76,000 was given to the Roberts Construction Company. This covered the excavations.

Ground was broken on May 25, 1923. The soil at the location is of clay and gravel sub-soil. For the most part, the construction is of concrete, reinforced and of the cantilever type.

There are two units of seats. The field runs north and south and the banks of seats are connected at the ends of a colonnade which will eventually form a continuous running track under cover.

The seating capacity is 40,000. With the balconies full length, one-fifth of the capacity is taken care of here. Each side is divided into seven sections with an acre of 80 feet on the outside. The forms used were standard and were used for all of the work with the exception of the ends which are true halves of the other sections.

The concrete work was done in a novel way. The mortar was mixed on the ground, hoisted to the top, and then by hopper cars running on a track laid on top of the structure to chutes which delivered the concrete to its proper place.

Detail of the east side of the stadium during construction. The concrete was hoisted up the tower, dumped into the cars and moved to the chutes where it was dumped.

Tracks laid about the stadium made it possible to shunt the gravel gondolas direct to the work from the railroad yards. This saved an extra handling, as the gravel was scooped directly out of the cars and into the mixing hopper.

According to the contractors, the feature of having the indoor track is a bit unusual. This is three feet above the field proper. Provision is being made for indoor baseball, football, tennis courts, etc., under the stands.

The concrete girders are 47 feet long, 8 feet high and 20 inches wide. This is the first time this sort of space has been utilized, according to reports.

Drainage of the field is assured by a sub-layer of cylinders 6 inches thick covering the whole playing area. These are augmented by catch basins 50 feet apart which empty into the storm sewer.

Mr. E.G. Hawkins was general superintendent of construction, Mr. K.J. Hawkins chief engineer and Mr. James Fiddock business manager of concrete work.

Dale R. Van Horn

AMERICAN BUILDER, November 1924.

Chapter Two

Enthusiasm Builds for Game Day

Why Memorial Stadium?

Let us all be mindful of the inscription which charges us to recognize those who made the ultimate sacrifice for God and Country...

"IN
COMMEMORATION
OF THE
MEN OF NEBRASKA
WHO SERVED
AND FELL
IN THE
NATIONS WARS"

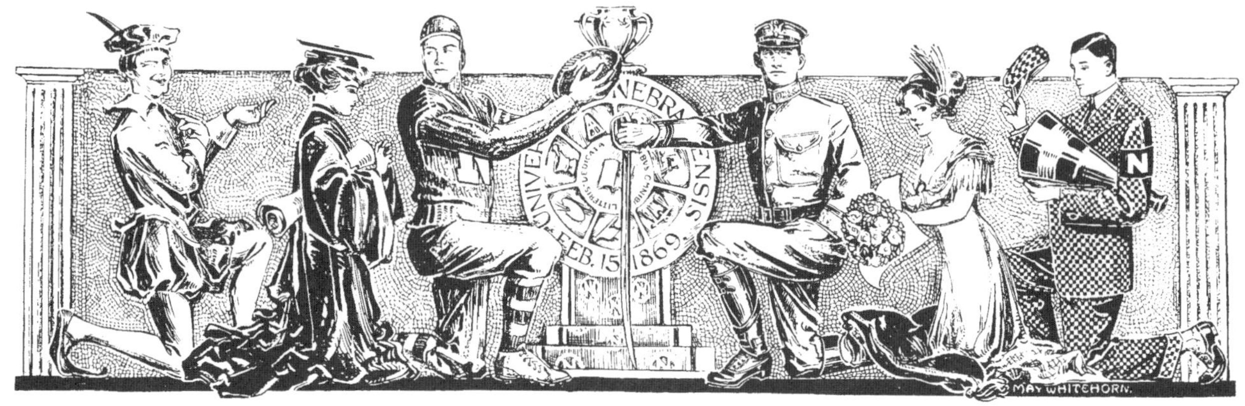

The Building Begins...

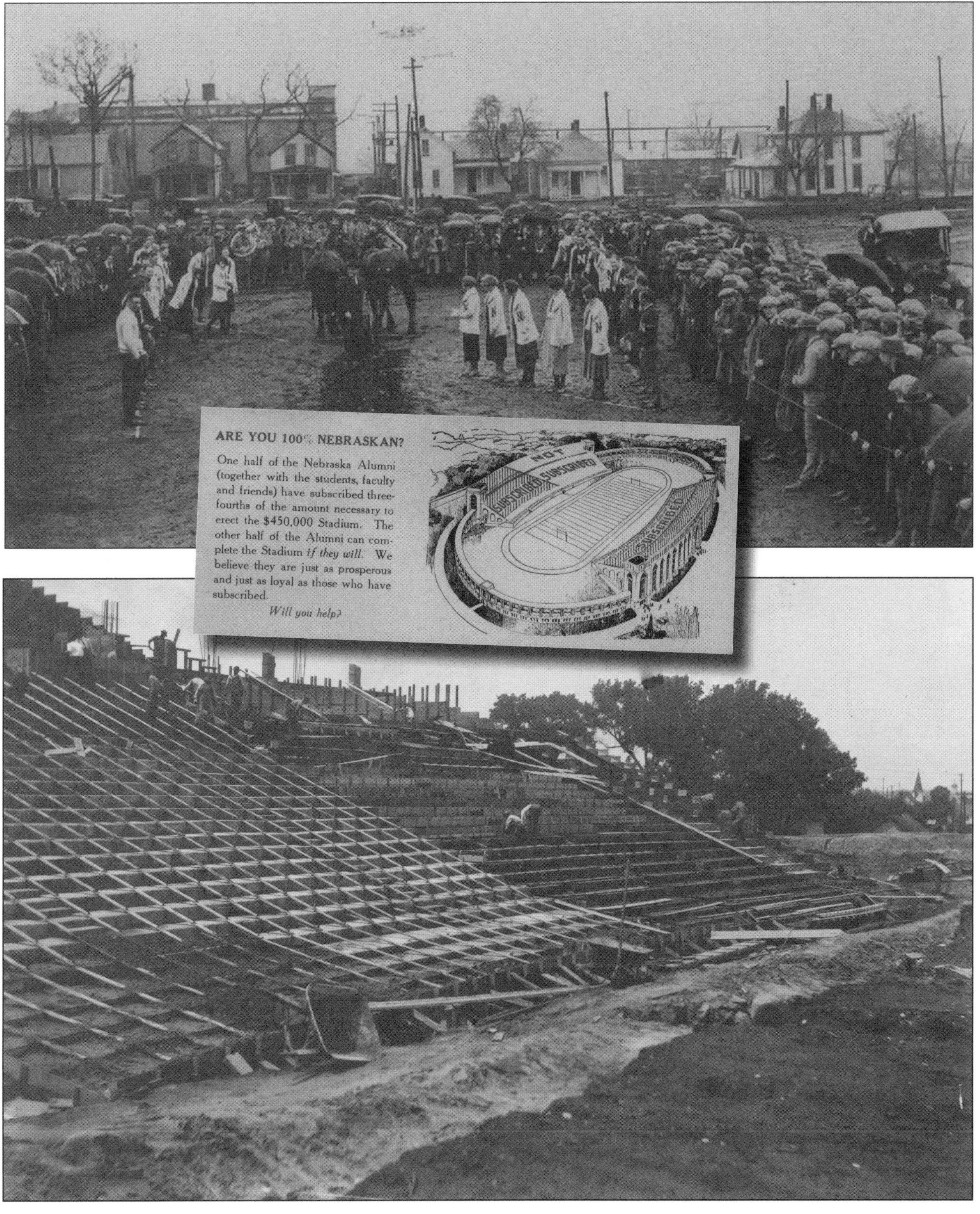

MEMORIAL · STADIUM
OF · THE · UNIVERSITY · OF
NEBRASKA · MCMXXIII

Profits from publication of program divided as follows:

50 per cent applies on Stadium indebtedness.
40 per cent accrues to trophy fund of Varsity N club.
10 per cent goes to corn-cobs, Nebraska's pep organization, who will sell the programs.

NIGHT SCENE STADIUM

UNIVERSITY OF NEBRASKA
1924
FOOTBALL PROGRAM

Published by
University of Nebraska Athletic Department

Prepared by H. D. Gish — Price 25c

Profits from publication of program divided as follows:
50 per cent applies on Stadium indebtedness.
40 per cent accrues to trophy fund of Varsity N club.
10 per cent goes to corn-cobs, Nebraska's pep organization, who will sell the programs.

BIRDSEYE VIEW OF STADIUM

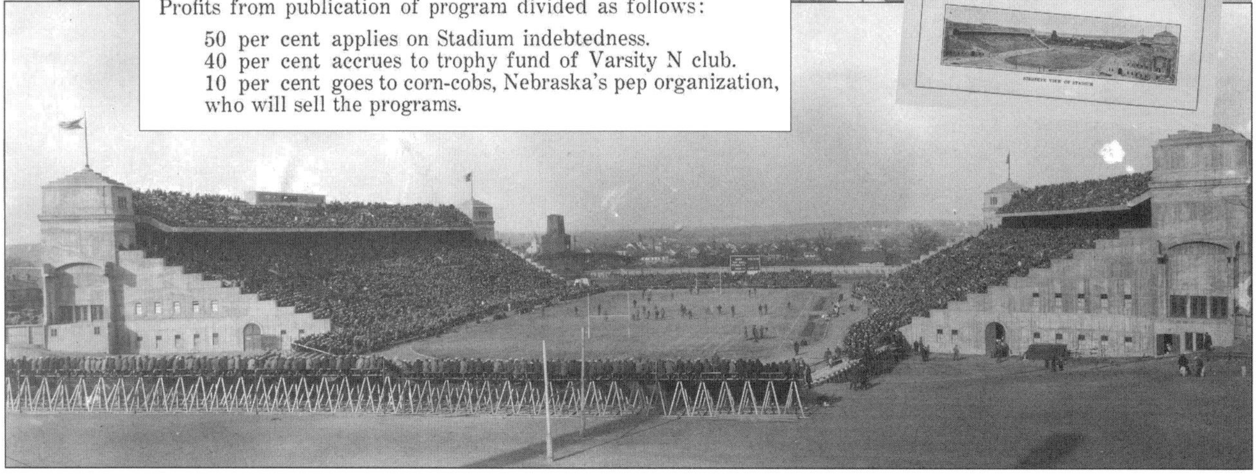

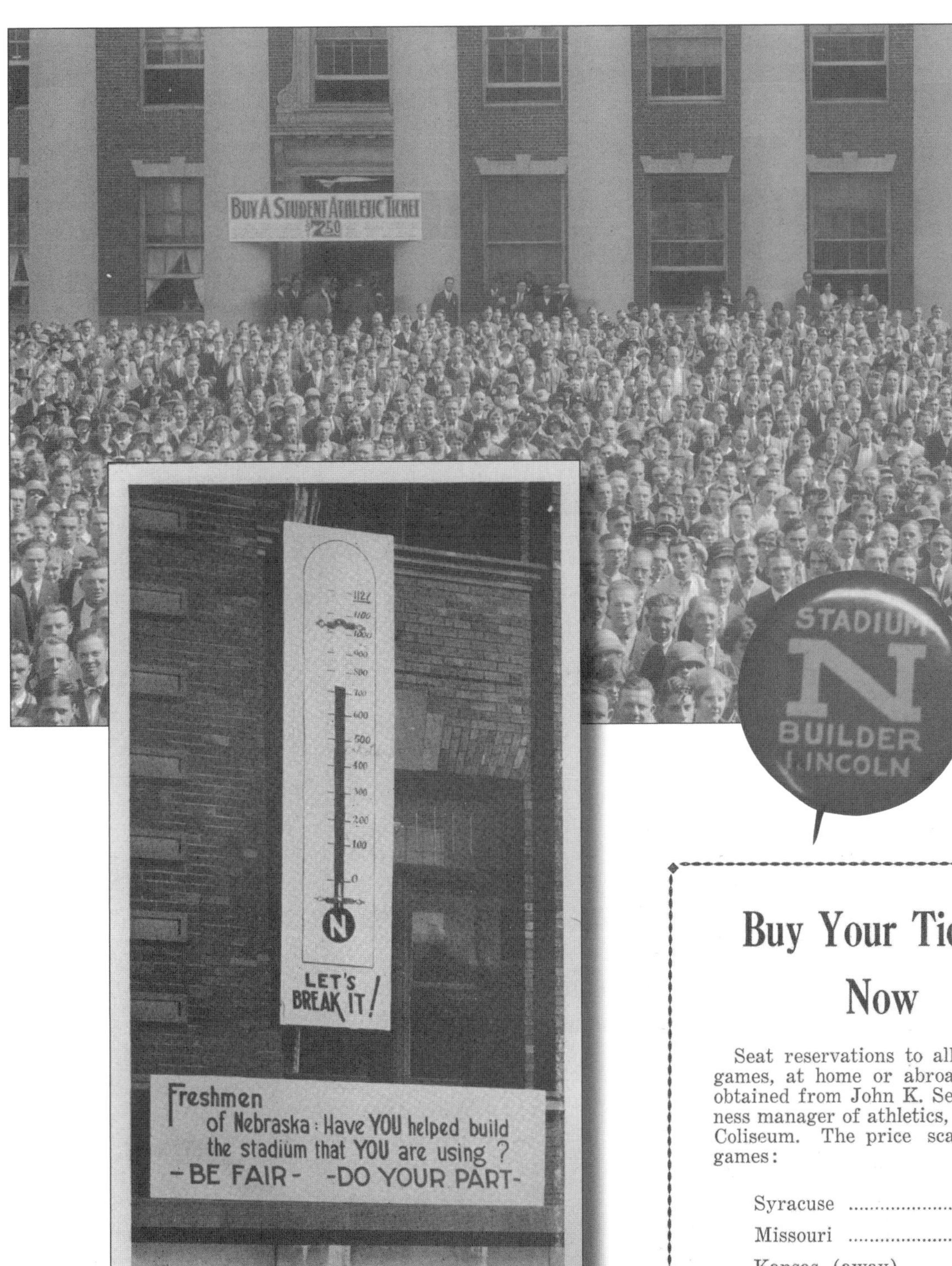

In 1924, the Freshmen Thermometer broke before the fundrasing campaign ended.

Buy Your Tickets Now

Seat reservations to all Nebraska games, at home or abroad, may be obtained from John K. Selleck, business manager of athletics, University Coliseum. The price scale for all games:

Syracuse	$2.50
Missouri	2.50
Kansas (away)	2.50
Oklahoma (away)	2.50
Pitt	2.50
Army (away)	4.00
Kansas Aggies	2.50

Order Your Tickets Today

Memorial Stadium

To get the desired three by four inch view of Nebraska's stadium a photographer might walk around it seven times and his pursuit would still be in vain, for it ovals away from him endlessly. One could get a pointblank shot at it from the air, but empty seats, even people enmasse, bundled in blankets, aren't as attractive as arched windows, which lend beauty to the mammoth structure.

The stadium, which holds 30,000 without the bleachers, is a memorial to University of Nebraska Men who have died in the nation's wars. The half million dollar cost was defrayed by students, faculty, alumni and friends. Many a tonsil shred ding joust has taken place within the stadium's great arms.

The following from the helpful typewriter of Walter Dobbins gives details: "The first game played on stadium sod was with the Oklahoma Sooners, October 13, 1923, just a week before dedication of the bowl. With its building Nebraska became a 'big time' football school. Games were scheduled with top flight teams from north, south, east and west. The largest crowd ever packed into the home field witnessed Nebraska's 7 to 0 victory over Indiana October 20, 1937.

"Some of Nebraska's gridiron triumphs have been recorded at the stadium, including the amazing 14 to 7 victory over Notre Dame's Four Horsemen in 1923; the 17 to 0 win over Rocknes' eleven in 1924 and the last of the 11 game series with the fighting Irish. New York's U's national title hopes were blasted on the same field in 1926 and 1927. Greatest of all victories, however, are later ones – the 14 to 9 defeat of Minnesota in 1937 and the 6-0 win over the Gophers in 1939."

Taken from Seeing Lincoln, issued by Gold & Co.
Written for the Nebraska State Journal
Ann Longman, ca. 1945

Dr. C. R. Richards speaks at Stadium Dedication in 1923.

A "Cutting-Edge" Precursor to the Instant Replay

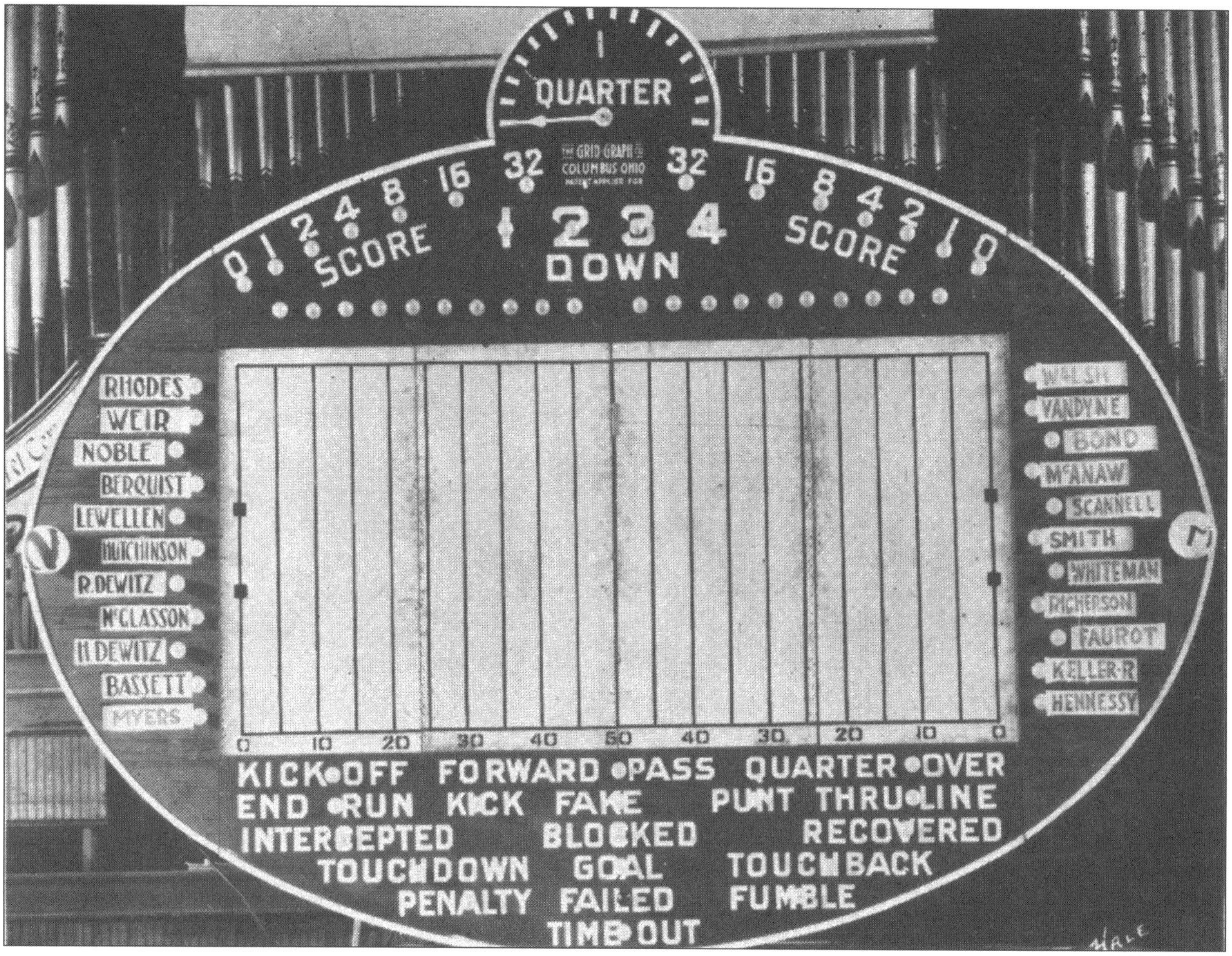

Gridograph in action for the Nebraska-Missouri game

Towards the latter part of the football season in 1923, a means was found by which larger crowds could watch the out-of-town football games. A scoreboard known as the Gridograph was invented and Nebraska rented one for the '23 season. The results were shown in the Armory at a twenty-five cent admission charge. It was doubtful, at first, if the plan would be successful, but the place was crowded every game.

The Gridograph was able to show the name of the player, the sort of movement or play, the yards gained, and the opponent who stopped the play. All this was done by a complicated mechanism of lights - a little red light darting across the sheet, which in turn was cut up into ten yard lines. In doing so, it showed the amount of gain or loss. Although this apparatus was not quite as interesting as the game, it aroused much enthusiasm.

GEE, TAKE A SQUINT AT THAT GOOD LOOKING GAL! LET'S LAND RIGHT HERE PETE I THINK SHE WANTS TO KNOW ME!
N
WHAT THEY SAW
YES I SAW HER UP IN MAGEE'S GREY ROOM DOLLIN' UP YESTERDAY—MOST OF THE SWELL DATES GET THEIR CLOTHES THERE—NO USE OF YOU SPOOFIN' HER IN THESE FLYIN' TOGS—WE'LL LAND DOWN AT MAGEE'S AND YOU DOLL YOURSELF UP IN A NEW ROYAL OXFORD SUIT—THEY'RE ACE HIGH FOR CORNHUSKERS!
Alan Kleitt
PEOPLE WHO WEAR CLOTHES FROM MAGEE'S STAND OUT FROM THE CROWD

"Three on the 50-yard Line For Tomorrow's Game"

Football in a modern university is more than a game-it is a spectacle. Today as you watch the Cornhuskers and Tigers in their all-important game, you see the finished product, an athletic picture which has been months in the making.

Even before the coaches have started the task of grooming the grid candidates, Business Manger of Athletics John. K. Selleck and his corps of assistants have been busy preparing the details and arrangements necessary for handling the throng which flocks to the Memorial stadium during a pigskin season.

The first task of course, is selling the tickets and the University ticket office never closes. Even now with the 1928 season not half completed, Mr. Selleck's office has on file numerous reservations for games on the 1929 schedule. The big rush starts in August and until the curtain rolls down Thanksgiving day, the coliseum office receives a steady stream of mail orders.

The mail order business is additional to the tickets sold over the counter at the coliseum and the two other offices – Latsch Brothers in Lincoln and Northrup-Jones Co., in Omaha.

One rule of the office, however, is that mail orders shall receive the same immediate attention given personal sales. Many football patrons are of the impression that they obtain better seats by ordering through Lincoln people, players on the varsity team or university students. This is not the case for no tickets are held in reserve and ordering through a third party generally means a delay of a day or more with the result that the tickets generally are not quite as good as if the order was placed direct with the business manager of athletics.

A total of more than 500 people are necessary to handle the crowd such as fills the stadium today. This group includes over 300 ushers, 24 ticket takers, eight ticket sellers, eight attendants for rest rooms, police force, guards, and a small regiment of managers and assistants that look after the field, dressing rooms, etc.

A strict audit is maintained over the finances of each game. The locked ticket boxes, in which the ticket-takers drop the stubs, are taken to the University finance office where six or seven men working the day after the game complete the audit, counting each ticket separately and placing it in its own classification.

Handling crowds is Mr. Selleck's specialty for in the winter he directs the seating for basketball games, athletic contests. Mr. Selleck's study of football crown psychology has brought many interesting deductions. Among other features he has found:

That the ideal stadium would be one a mile high with all the seats on the 50-yard line, for a majority of last-minute purchaser are surprised when they find the 40-yard line seats all gone the day of the game.

That if Nebraska wins, no one complains about the location of his ticket.

That many times the seats on the goal line are the ones of real value. For example, last week goal line seats to the north would have been the ideal situation to watch both touchdowns,

That cold or rainy weather find many people searching around for reason why they should not be permitted inside the glass-enclosed press box.

That the public's ideas of a good seat is gradually changing. When the stadium was first built the rush was for seats near the field. Now they want to get 25 or 30 rows up and are gradually learning that the best seats are in the balcony.

That many people save their ticket stubs and send them in to buy the same position next season.

That block reservations are growing larger each year, indication that Nebraska football games are now a social event with party groups making the games a get-together affair.

Along with the usual barrage of ticket orders, Mr. Selleck's mail includes a number of odd requests and comments. Here's a sample selected from this week's correspondence:

"Mr. Selleck :Each season I order tickets a week before the day of the game. Each year I receive worse tickets. How do you explain this?"

A mother writes: "Mr. Selleck please send me a Pittsburgh ticket. I purchased one last week but same was destroyed by playing children. The seat was on the west side."

Here's one that arrived the day before the Syracuse game: "Please reserve me one seat on the 50-yard line. I will call for it tomorrow."

And another that came in early and was turned over to the mathematicians: "I want two tickets to the Missouri game. I want them in the center of the field about half way up. But if you can't get them half way up then put them down near the sidelines. If they are in the balcony get them in the first row. If there are none available in the west stand get them about in the 20th row on the east side. If you think it will rain, I would appreciate them under the balcony. If you can't get them together send me one good seat and one anywhere as I am bringing my wife and she don't know much about football. P.S. Make that three tickets as her mother has decided to come along."

Gregg McBride

"Howl"-arious depiction of the 1928 Homecoming clash between the Mizzou Tigers (featured as actual tigers, complete with tails) and the Nebraska Cornhuskers.

Note Selleck carting a wheelbarrow full of money down the sidelines, and Husker photographer of record, MacDonald, capturing all the action on the field of play.

RICHARDS
M.C. MUMMA
E
AMES
MC MULLEN
FARLEY
SLOAN
SCHULTE
HOLM
HOWELL
BEARG
LEWANDOWSKI
GISH
HAWKINS
McLEAN
DR.
EVERETT
PROGRAM
LEWIS
SELLECK
N
Nebraska
versus
Missouri
HOMECOMING
1928

Husker Homecoming Happenings

In 1911, the Junior-Senior Prom committee saw the necessity of some kind of a day to bring alumni back to Nebraska. This committee announced the first Homecoming Day a short time after the close of the football season. The next year the Athletic Department was given charge of Homecoming Day for Nebraska. To give the Alumni an opportunity to see the football team in action the second Homecoming Day was announced for the date of the Michigan game in 1912. From that time up to the present date the annual Homecoming Day had been held on the date of some important football game. Thus, alumni come back to Nebraska every year, come for hundreds of miles, to see old friends, to view again the buildings, and to observe the changes that take place from year to year.

No Homecoming bonfire happened without a lot of preparation. As you can see from the height of the pylons in this photo, the construction-heaping process still had a ways to go before the glow would be seen by the scores of folks in attendance later that evening (note glow of fire at right in photo above). Citing safety concerns, the University has since discontinued the tradition.

Stadium Facts and Figures

East Stadium, Uni. of Nebr. Lincoln 8/18/24

The Nebraska Memorial stadium, in which the Cornhuskers play their home games has a permanent seating capacity of 30,000 which with the addition of temporary bleachers can handle a crowd of 47,000.

There are four rows of seats in the box section with a seating capacity of 992; the main section has 47 rows with a seating capacity of 22,338; the balcony section has fifteen rows with a seating capacity of 6,770.

The overall length of the stadium is 760 feet, the width 551 feet. The length of each stand is 476 feet (over one and one-half city blocks), the width of each stand is 136 feet (about half a city block), the height of the stadium is 72 feet (six story building). The lineal length of seats is 8.52 miles. The circumference of the cinder track is 440 yards with a quarter-mile stretch with but one turn.

Twenty-two ramps feed forty-eight aisles, thus insuring rapid handling of capacity crowds. A regiment of four hundred ushers is required to handle a capacity crowd.

Actual construction of the stadium began May 25th 1923. It is expected to be fully completed including the indoor training plant, by December 15, 1924.

The stadium is used for many purposes other than the staging of athletic contests.

In the two tower sections of the east stand, on the ground level, are locker and shower rooms which will accommodate eight hundred athletes. All outdoor sport teams such as football, track, baseball and cross country are now using these dressing rooms.

Under the east stand will be found a seven-lap-to-the-mile running track where Coach Henry F. Schulte will train his "Five hundred men out for track."

The west stadium stand houses the stores and job system of the university. This includes printing, electrical, carpenter, plumbing, traffic and repair shops as well as the stores and job system offices.

This summer the stadium was used for public gatherings of a national nature. The public address system, installed in the stadium, made it possible for the speaker to be heard in all parts of the stadium. The Governor C.W. Bryan notification ceremony and Charles G. Dawes opening campaign speech were successfully staged in the stadium.

The stadium will probably be used for pageants and all alumni Round-up festivities next May and June.

University of Nebraska Football Program
Homecoming Game
October 18, 1924

Chapter Three

Game Day Advances

First Team got the Lower Berths

In his Senior year, on a trip by train to play Oregon State, Ron Douglas remembers there were six private cars. So casual was the itinerary, that on the return trip, the train actually made a stop at Glacier National Park to allow each player to cut down his own Christmas Tree.

In the 30s, the team wore leather helmets, had no training table and voted on whether to travel out of town to a game, based on how much school work was due the following week. A tidbit which should, no doubt, make the heart of any academic heap praises on the game of football at that time. Legendary Coach D. X. Bible was at the helm, choosing a captain for each game, Ron being his choice for the Pittsburgh game. He says the crowds were good and loud, with rallies occurring the night before a game. There was, in fact, so much commotion at his fraternity on those evenings, that he chose to check into a room at the Cornhusker Hotel to secure a good night's sleep.

At age 95, he still enjoys game days and a stirring round of golf with the current football team.

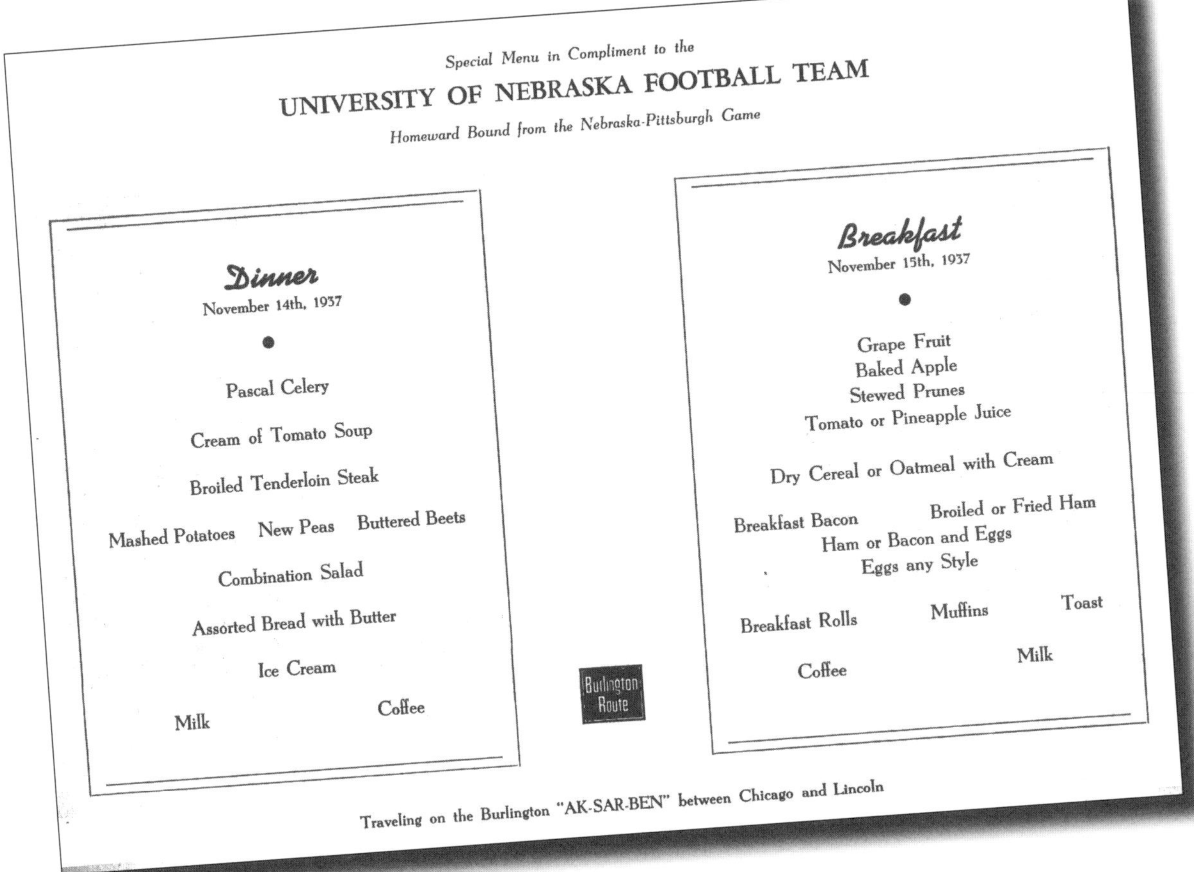

Special Menu in Compliment to the

UNIVERSITY OF NEBRASKA FOOTBALL TEAM

Homeward Bound from the Nebraska-Pittsburgh Game

Dinner
November 14th, 1937

Pascal Celery

Cream of Tomato Soup

Broiled Tenderloin Steak

Mashed Potatoes New Peas Buttered Beets

Combination Salad

Assorted Bread with Butter

Ice Cream

Milk Coffee

Burlington Route

Breakfast
November 15th, 1937

Grape Fruit
Baked Apple
Stewed Prunes
Tomato or Pineapple Juice

Dry Cereal or Oatmeal with Cream

Breakfast Bacon Broiled or Fried Ham
Ham or Bacon and Eggs
Eggs any Style

Breakfast Rolls Muffins Toast

Coffee Milk

Traveling on the Burlington "AK-SAR-BEN" between Chicago and Lincoln

ITINERARY

University of Nebraska Football Team
Oregon State Game at Portland
November 28, 1936

Wednesday, November 25

9:30 A.M.	Leave Lincoln via Union Pacific from Burlington Station
12:00 M.	Lunch on Diner
4:00 P.M.(C.T.)	Arrive North Platte Detrain for practice
4:30 P.M.(M.T.)	Leave North Platte
6:00 P.M.	Dinner on Diner

Thursday, November 26

8:00 A.M.	Breakfast on Diner (In Idaho)
12:00 M.	Lunch on Diner
4:00 P.M.	Arrive Boise (Capital of Idaho) Detrain for practice
5:30 P.M.	Leave Boise
6:00 P.M.	Dinner on Diner

Friday, November 27

8:00 A.M.	Breakfast on Diner
8:30 A.M.	Arrive Bonneville Dam Detrain and take motor coach along Columbia River Highway via Multnomah Falls
9:30 A.M.	Leave Bonneville Dam by motor coach
11:20 A.M.	Arrive Portland Team will stop at the Multnomah Hotel, Portland
12:00 M.	Lunch with Nebraska alumni
Friday Afternoon	Practice and sight-seeing trip
6:00 P.M.	Dinner
7:00 P.M.	Picture Show
10:00 P.M.	Lights out

Saturday, November 28

8:00 A.M.	Breakfast
11:00 A.M.	Lunch
2:00 P.M.	Kick-off
5:30 P.M.	Dinner
11:30 P.M.	Leave Portland, Union Station via Northern Pacific

Sunday, November 29

6:45 A.M.	Arrive Seattle, King Street Station Cars will be set out for occupancy until 7:45
8:00 A.M.	Breakfast in King Street Station
8:30 A.M.	Leave by bus from King Street Station for Coleman Dock
8:45 A.M.	Leave Coleman Dock by Ferry for Bremerton Navy Yard

Sunday, November 29, continued

11:00 A.M.	Leave Bremerton Navy Yard by Ferry for Seattle
12:20 P.M.	Leave Coleman Dock for Olympic Hotel
12:45 P.M.	Lunch - Olympic Hotel
2:00 P.M.	Leave Olympic Hotel for sight-seeing trip of Seattle and University of Washington
4:30 P.M.	Arrive King Street Station
5:00 P.M.	Leave Seattle, King Street Station via Great Northern Railway
5:30 P.M.	Dinner on Diner

Monday, November 30

8:00 A.M.	Breakfast on Diner
12:00 M.	Lunch on Diner
12:30 P.M.	Detrain for motor trip to foot of Lake McDonald in Glacier National Park
1:30 P.M.	Leave Belton
3:30 P.M.	Arrive Glacier Park Station. Detrain for hike to Glacier Park Hotel and visit to Mike's Frontier Place
5:30 P.M.	Leave Glacier Park Station via Great Northern Railway
6:00 P.M.	Dinner on Diner

Tuesday, December 1

5:00 A.M.	Arrive Billings
5:00 A.M.	Leave Billings, Burlington Railway for Lincoln
8:00 A.M.	Breakfast on Diner
12:00 M.	Lunch on Diner
6:00 P.M.	Dinner on Diner

Arrive Lincoln sometime after midnight

If very late, cars will be set out for those desiring to occupy sleepers for the night. Breakfast will be served at Burlington Station

THE HUSKERS HAVE NO TRAINING TABLE

YOU CAN MEET THEM ANY DAY AT THE CENTRAL, THAT'S THE ANSWER

Central Hotel

PRESNELL

Central Cafe

Where the Gang Meet, Greet and Eat

Extreamly Clean

1325 P Street — Lincoln, Nebraska

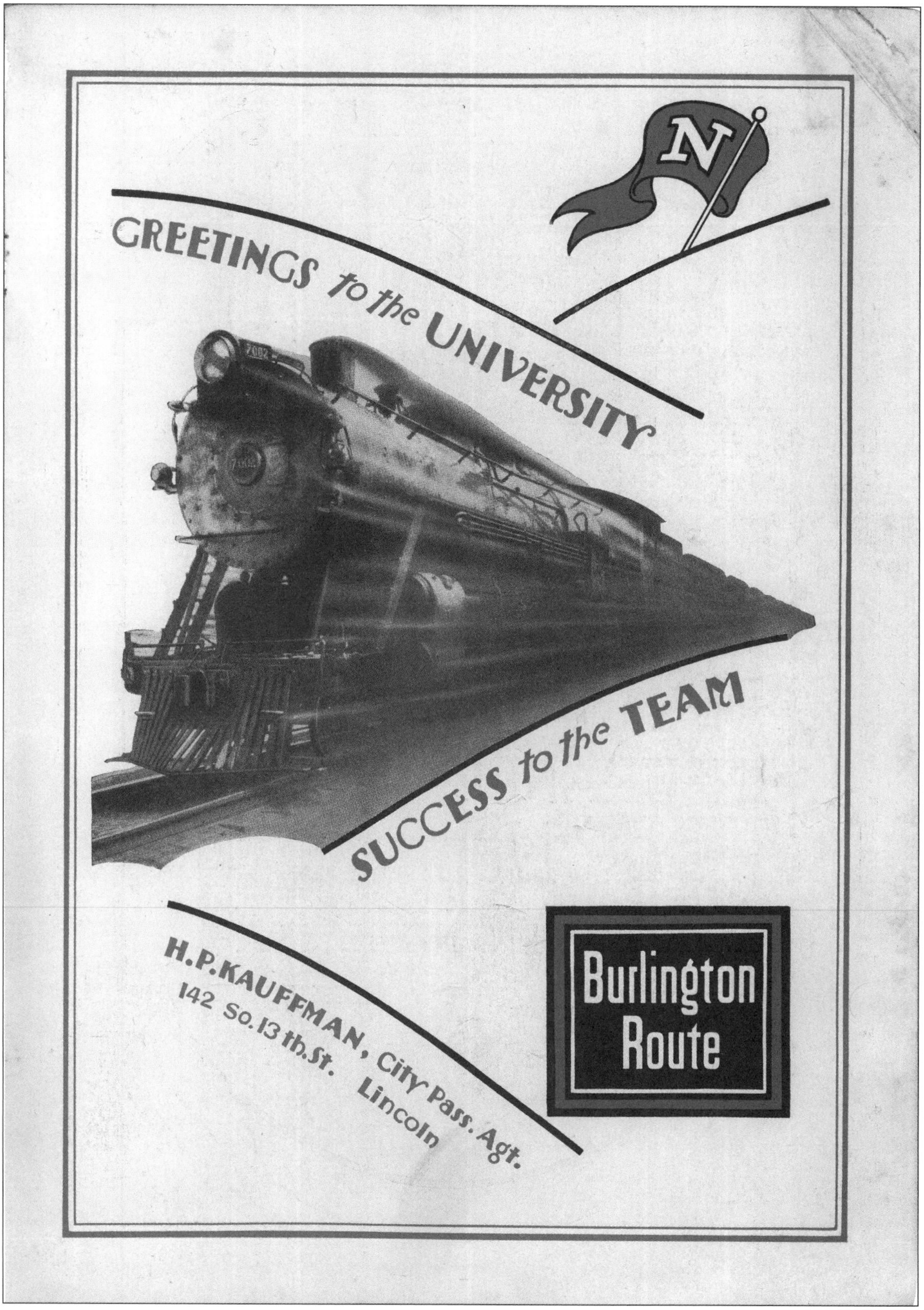

N

GREETINGS to the UNIVERSITY

SUCCESS to the TEAM

H.P. KAUFFMAN, City Pass. Agt.
142 So. 13 th. St. Lincoln

Burlington
Route

WHEN THE TEAM IS AWAY

and it looks like you are going to miss a football game, just limber up the old antenna and listen to a play-by-play account of the game on a Crosley or a Amrad receiver.

Broadcast by

Nebraska Buick Automobile Co.

RADIO STATION

K - F - A - B

During the football season play-by-play reports of all Nebraska games can be heard through Nebraska Buick's new super-power station.

Listen in on KFAB for all the football dope!

After the Game
Drop in the

LINCOLN
LUNCH
ROOM

The HOTEL
LINCOLN

250 Rooms   Rates From $1.50   150 Baths

Two Nebraska football players and their girlfriends pose for throngs of admirers outside of the Varsity theater near 13th & P Streets sometime in the 1930s.

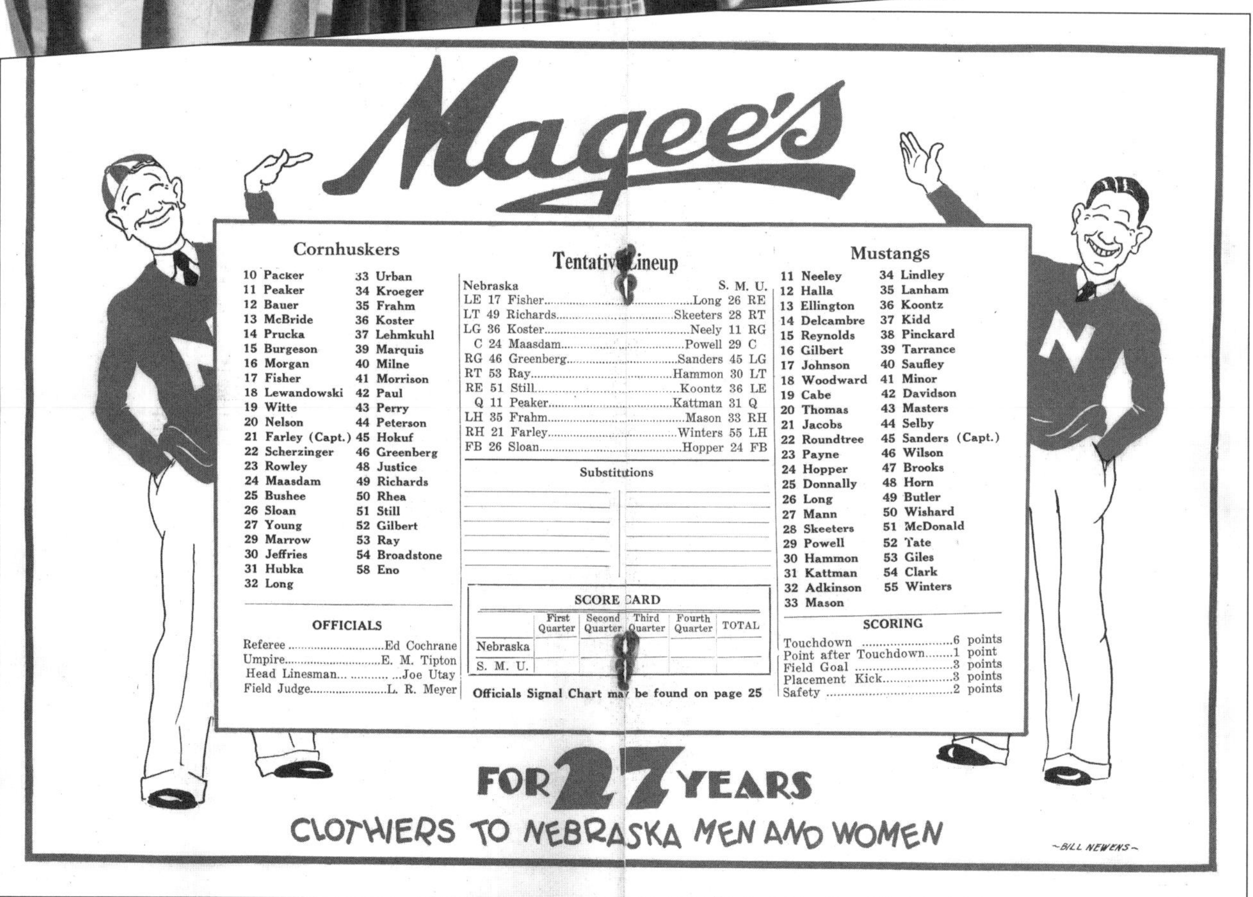

Magee's

Cornhuskers

10 Packer
11 Peaker
12 Bauer
13 McBride
14 Prucka
15 Burgeson
16 Morgan
17 Fisher
18 Lewandowski
19 Witte
20 Nelson
21 Farley (Capt.)
22 Scherzinger
23 Rowley
24 Maasdam
25 Bushee
26 Sloan
27 Young
29 Marrow
30 Jeffries
31 Hubka
32 Long
33 Urban
34 Kroeger
35 Frahm
36 Koster
37 Lehmkuhl
39 Marquis
40 Milne
41 Morrison
42 Paul
43 Perry
44 Peterson
45 Hokuf
46 Greenberg
48 Justice
49 Richards
50 Rhea
51 Still
52 Gilbert
53 Ray
54 Broadstone
58 Eno

OFFICIALS

Referee ....Ed Cochrane
Umpire............................E. M. Tipton
Head Linesman... ....Joe Utay
Field Judge.......................L. R. Meyer

Tentative Lineup

Nebraska	S. M. U.
LE 17 Fisher	Long 26 RE
LT 49 Richards	Skeeters 28 RT
LG 36 Koster	Neely 11 RG
C 24 Maasdam	Powell 29 C
RG 46 Greenberg	Sanders 45 LG
RT 53 Ray	Hammon 30 LT
RE 51 Still	Koontz 36 LE
Q 11 Peaker	Kattman 31 Q
LH 35 Frahm	Mason 33 RH
RH 21 Farley	Winters 55 LH
FB 26 Sloan	Hopper 24 FB

Substitutions

SCORE CARD

	First Quarter	Second Quarter	Third Quarter	Fourth Quarter	TOTAL
Nebraska					
S. M. U.					

Officials Signal Chart may be found on page 25

Mustangs

11 Neeley
12 Halla
13 Ellington
14 Delcambre
15 Reynolds
16 Gilbert
17 Johnson
18 Woodward
19 Cabe
20 Thomas
21 Jacobs
22 Roundtree
23 Payne
24 Hopper
25 Donnally
26 Long
27 Mann
28 Skeeters
29 Powell
30 Hammon
31 Kattman
32 Adkinson
33 Mason
34 Lindley
35 Lanham
36 Koontz
37 Kidd
38 Pinckard
39 Tarrance
40 Saufley
41 Minor
42 Davidson
43 Masters
44 Selby
45 Sanders (Capt.)
46 Wilson
47 Brooks
48 Horn
49 Butler
50 Wishard
51 McDonald
52 Tate
53 Giles
54 Clark
55 Winters

SCORING

Touchdown ....6 points
Point after Touchdown........1 point
Field Goal ....3 points
Placement Kick....................3 points
Safety ....2 points

FOR 27 YEARS
CLOTHIERS TO NEBRASKA MEN AND WOMEN

—BILL NEWENS—

Falling Hard for the Huskers

I fell hard for the Cornhuskers as a nine-year old in 1934. The first game that I watched was against Wyoming and we won big. Knothole tickets were 10 cents, and you could bring your own food and drink

1935 was even better when we beat the first Heisman Trophy winner, Jay Berwanger, 28 to 6, and our Jerry LaNoue looked better than Jay that day. The next year Sam Francis and Lloyd Cardwell and all the team outplayed the national champion Gophers in Minneapolis only to lose 7-0. We continued to win regularly in Biff Jones' first year 1937, but along came Paul Christman and Missouri to out-score us in 1938 and 1939. I managed to enter the Missouri locker room, after the 1940 game, and secure Paul's autograph. Nebraska got some revenge that day, and eventually a Rose Bowl trip at the end of the season.

Some of us sneaked past the guard after most home games, to talk to the players in the NU locker room, and walk back with them to their fraternities. In 1936, Right Guard Lowell English had an old convertible and we'd ride with him. He became a major general in the Marines during WW2. All the players were incredibly kind to us. My hero worship continues to this day for those guys. They played for the fun and love of the game, in the best traditional school spirit of the 1930s.

I attended every game possible throughout my time in Lincoln, except when I worked Saturday afternoons in 1942, at Dolton's Luncheonette on 13th Street, just south of the Stuart. I envied all the fans who passed by on their way to the game, which started at 2:00 P.M. in those days. Sometimes the game ended in the twilight of late November. My memories of that era, and NU football, continue to shine brightly.

Frank Mulvey

"Brother, can you spare a dime?"

In my job as a photographer for a local printing firm, I sometimes found myself inside the Russ's Market at 17th & Washington Street. A host of elders have graciously approached me there from time to time to tell me how much they love the Peeking contest we do in the Neighborhood Extra, or perhaps to give us kudos for a show we've done for a Brownbaggers lunch at the Museum of Nebraska History, or for an evening show we might have done in recent past at a retirement community.

On one occasion, a gentleman who worked there named Pete Debus came forward to shake my hand. Pete is a very affable fellow with a great sense of humor and an inquisitive mind. "When's the next book coming out?" He asked. "Fall of next year, Pete." I replied, "Got any good memories you want to share about Nebraska football or a game day memory of some kind?" Pete rubbed his chin and then said, "Well, just one, I guess...there was this game at Memorial Stadium... it was Homecoming... I think we were playing the Missouri Tigers... it might be an interesting story... but I'm not real proud of my behavior on that particular day."

I knew in my heart that he had a good story to tell even before he began to speak.

He began to tell me of a time in the 30s when money was scarce. Even scarcer if you were a kid. Pete found himself down on O street on a Saturday morning in the Fall, wishing he had the dime it would take to get him a seat in the knothole section at Memorial Stadium for that day's game. But there simply wasn't much of a chance he'd come up with one unless he found it lying on the sidewalk. Wandering near 20th and O, he was just outside of Messner's Auto Supply when a thought occurred to him. If he couldn't find a dime, perhaps he could make one. He scrounged around looking for odd discards of hardware along the train tracks. A nut here, a washer there. A few small items found there way onto one of the rails. A passing train would take care of the rest.

Sure enough, when the next train had passed, an acorn nut he had placed there was squashed into (roughly) the diameter of a dime.

The only thing left to do was to head for the stadium and see if the ruse might take hold. He waited patiently for a crowd of kids to form in front of the man at the gate wearing a carpenter's apron. As the kids marched through single file, the man checked their IDs and held the apron open to receive their admittance for the game. Pete took up a position at the rear and gingerly flipped the slug into his pouch. His heart pounded a little faster, but as Pete held up his ID card, the slug tapped out its compliance with the gatekeeper's request. The man's watchful eyes seemed to stay on the horizon, keeping track of the kids who were behind Pete. He was, as they used to say, "in like Flynn."

Pete's voice suddenly changed, luring me out of the vivid canvas he had just painted. "Like I say," he said, "not one of my proudest moments."

I assured Pete that the statute of limitations had most certainly run out on his crime, and that the Good Lord would graciously forgive any little boy such a transgression...especially at a point in our country's history when commodities of all kinds were pretty hard to come by.

Jon Roth/Pete Debus

The Knothole Gang

In the 1930s Nebraska's football stadium had no seating in the north and south ends. The Schulte Field House was on the north end and as times were hard, there were plenty of empty seats. So, they put bleachers in the south end and called it the Knothole Section. They let us kids in with an ID card and ten cents.

Don Beck, Stan Miller and I went regularly. Our parents took turns taking us. NU was in the Big 6 then. Later Colorado joined and made it the Big 7, then Oklahoma State, to make it the Big 8. Finally, the Texas teams made it the Big 12.

The first game that I ever saw was NU versus Baylor. NU won, 26 – 14. They were Big 6 champs. The star halfback was Herman Rohrig, my favorite player. Back then, the quarterback wasn't as important as he is today. The ball was mostly centered directly to the halfbacks and fullback. The QB was a blocking back. Not many passes were thrown.

They ran a single wing offense and most of the players played both offense and defense. They didn't have scholarships – they really were "student athletes".

After a couple of seasons, they raised the price to a quarter. And when they started filling the stadium, that was the end of the Knothole Gang.

This is from "Farm Boy", a book of memoirs my wife put together for our family. I was born on the Wittstruck homestead at Centerville in 1925. Wittstruck Road and Wittstruck Creek were named for my pioneer great-grandparents – Julius and Mary Ann. I'm still a big Cornhusker fan.

Dwayne Wittstruck, 84

Cornhusker Plays Once Were Telegraphed

A slightly built gentleman, perhaps a bit past middle age, strode into the old second-floor Lincoln Journal newsroom and headed into the northwest corner, which was home to the sports department. The man placed his equipment on a desk and quickly hooked it up to a telegraph line to Memorial Stadium. It was, I soon learned, an annual ritual of uncertain origin. I can't recall the date of its ending, but there he was – a telegrapher in the sports department. The year was 1941.

It was a typical Nebraska autumn afternoon. Game days were busy ones in a newsroom. The first of six game-day editions had pre-game stories. The regular edition for streets sales followed. Then came a southeast Nebraska edition, a city edition and another street sales edition, soon revamped with a complete Cornhusker game story.

Lincoln's downtown was jammed with automobiles, directed by skilled and often portly arm waving, whistle-equipped traffic cops, at such busy intersections as 13th and O and 10th and O Streets. The University of Nebraska Cornhuskers were playing a major foe in Memorial Stadium – a mere 18 years old at that time.

The telegrapher in the sports department was linked to a counterpart in the wooden press box atop the west stadium. It was a perch with no amenities for sportswriters from Nebraska, the visiting team's home state and, on occasion, big circulation newspapers from across the nation.

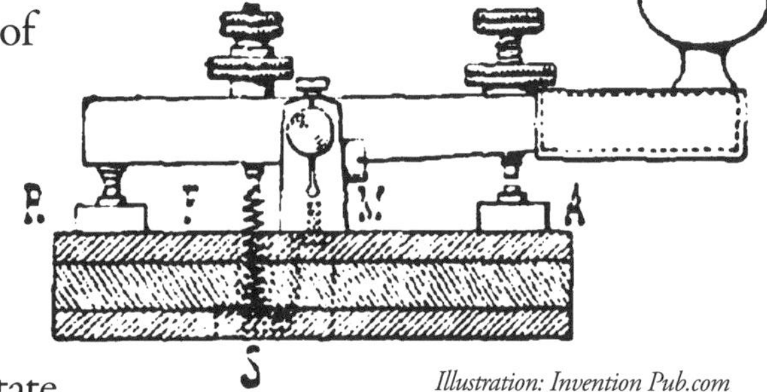

Illustration: Invention Pub.com

In those pre-television, pre-computer laptop days, the well-equipped sports writer's tool was his portable typewriter. Alongside some reporters were telegraphers who were handed play-by-play accounts quickly typed by writers as the game progressed. Back in the newsroom the receiving telegrapher deftly typed the Morse code account that, to a layman, was nothing more than the rapid clickety, click of the receiving machine.

Yes, indeed, the Cornhusker plays used to be telegraphed. Nothing to worry about, however, they had already been executed and the results known. Standing by in the newsroom was a "copy boy" who carried the typed copy to the composing room where it would be set into lead type by skilled Linotype operators, proof-read and placed into page forms.

Other preparations had been made. Large, black headline type was ready to scream any one of three ways a game could go – Cornhuskers Win, Opponents Win, or a tie game. No overtime to break a tie back in those days. Also the potential leads to the game story were set in advance, minus the final score, but ready for quick additions – win, lose or draw.

All this was before Husker Nation was created. But there was the Cornhusker band, Corncobs and Tassels and a heavy emphasis on Scarlet and Cream.

Up in the press box were such legendary writers as Cy Sherman, sports editor of the Lincoln Star, John Bentley and Walt Dobbins of the Lincoln Journal. Sherman is credited with labeling the Nebraska team as Cornhuskers, but that occurred while he was on the Journal sports staff.

Cornhusker fans of old wanted mementoes. And they wanted them fast! Back in the newspaper plant everyone was geared up to meet that demand. Stories flowed from the newsroom to the composing room. Stereotypers were ready to press cardboard-like material against pages of type to create a matrix. That matrix was placed into a curved device and molten metal was poured against the matrix to create a printing plate to go on a high-speed rotary newspaper press. Pressmen were at the ready. And so were all the people who would distribute newspapers as they poured from the press. All other pages of the newspaper, except the front page, were already locked onto the press.

We didn't always time how fast these last steps could be performed; yet one stands out. From game's end to press start was seven minutes as a result of a finely tuned cooperative effort. With the press cranked up to high-speed, newsboys were able to deliver newspapers with the complete play-by-play of the game as rabid Cornhusker fans exited Memorial Stadium. All that in "the good old days."

My first venture into Memorial Stadium was via a knothole ticket – 10 cents in the late 1920s. We kids watched the Cornhuskers whip a good Missouri team that was so pumped up those big guys left the field crying. It was the first time I saw grown men shed tears over a sports event. Little did I realize that years later I would be involved in helping cover Nebraska football.

George Round, probably the university's first public relations guy, was a good friend. It was rare for me to get away from work, but when I could, I called George. We'd exchanged pleasantries and then I'd tell him we would like to see the game Saturday.

"Sure, Gil, how many tickets?"

"Well, just my wife and I and the four kids."

"Great, stop by my office on your way to the stadium."

How about west stadium, 20 rows up, 40-yard line, and free tickets? We were always glad to perform this community service -- helping to cheer the Cornhuskers when the stadium capacity was 40,000 and there were many empty seats.

Photo: Textually.org

Gil Savery

Photo: Mary Jane Nielsen

Just A Tip

You will want to see the Nebraska Cornhuskers in action next season. If you like the seat location you now have, save the ticket stub and ask for the location next season.

If you think there is some other location which you might like, take a few minutes today after the game to see just how the field will look from some of these other seats. It may be that you would prefer a balcony ticket. You know there are a lot of "dyed in the wool" fans who would not think of sitting in any other place. There has been talk at times about the advisability of the coaches and team being seated in the upper section of the stadium. Distance to the field has been a serious drawback. It's a matter of opinion. The idea is to make your choice before it is too late.

Place your order now for 1931 tickets. Make sure of an excellent seat by placing your reservation now with Business Manager of Athletics John K. Selleck, Coliseum, University of Nebraska. Requests will be filled next fall in the order they are received. Don't wait. Do it NOW!

Ad Reprint: Tales of the Cornhuskers

NEBRASKA HOLDS THE CARDS

A Rah! Rah! Without an Echo

Dad and his gang gave 'em three cheers, but the Cornhuskers of today don't bother with cheers—they say it with cards. Three is a measly little number, so they just make it nine hundred and call it a day. Whether it be a welcome for National American Legion Commander O'Neil, a handshake for Dad, or a twist of the Tiger's tail, those nine hundred Cornhuskers are there and over. Led this year by Alan Williams of the Innocents Society, the section has made a very fine showing. A trip to Kansas where the Nebraskans gave the Jayhawk crowd a stunt or two, was the high spot of this year's performances.

The Nebraska cheering section stunts have become a feature that has grown to be an enjoyable part of every home game.

"Call by...er...ah...for Philip Morris!"

Ad Reprints: Tales of the Cornhuskers

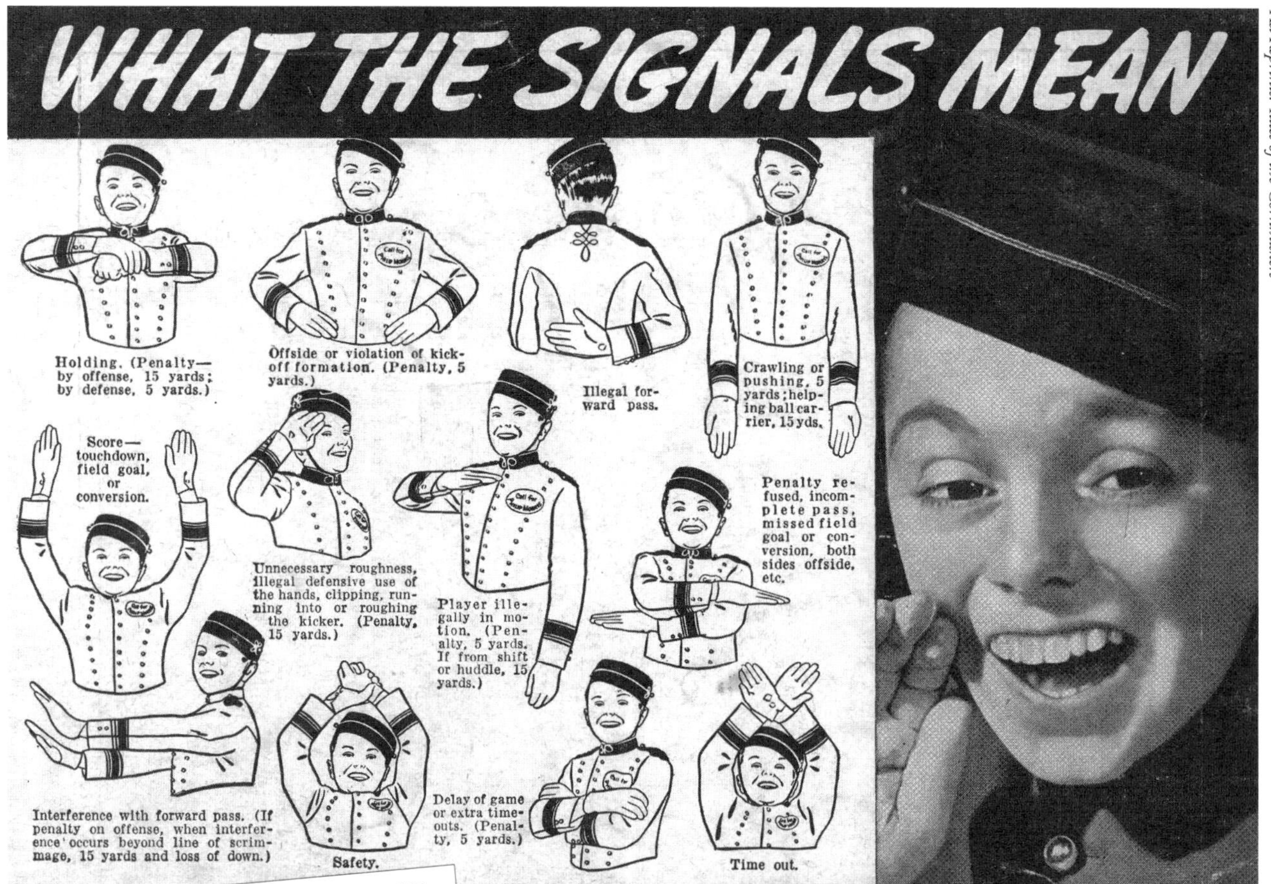

The famous Philip Morris Bellhop does his stand-up routine at the radio studios of KOLN in Lincoln. Photo courtesy of Bob & Sharon Hitz.

Photo: Davis & Wilson Photo Illustration: Tales of the Cornhuskers

Here Comes the Band

The entrance of the band on the field is a great moment in our greatest outdoor spectacle. Lacking a band, the spectacle loses much of its color and glamour. The band and its maneuvers are easily understood and appreciated by the large crowds which attend our games. The band owes to itself, to the institution it represents, and to the public the finest exhibition possible to add to the enjoyment of the day.

Few persons realize the amount of work involved in presenting a performance such as is to be seen today. After the general theme and sequence of the performance has been planned, the music must be arranged; the charting for each individual's movements are drafted; and the whole show must be minutely timed and correlated.

The Varsity marching unit this year is 9x12 man formation. Each man has a position number such as A1, C3, etc. On the field each bandsman's movements are governed by this number which charts his different positions.

A miniature football field is used in charting all formation in order that the proper perspective be ascertained and that easy understanding of the design be assured. The field is marked by squares representing the normal band step of 26 inches. From the setup on this field a master chart is made corresponding to the field positions, and from this each bandsman receives a chart covering his individual movements. The men are schooled in the reading of these charts at the beginning of the year so with few words of explanation, the new formation is ready to take form. This method makes possible the presenting of an entirely new feature at each game. All movements are designed along military lines to insure precision. The formations are planned to move as rapidly as possible with no breaks in either the music or the continuity of motion. Accuracy and coordination in timing between music and motion is the big problem.

Twirlers are used as assistant drum majors and key point men throughout the formations.

The band rehearses daily from 5 to 6 o'clock in the afternoon. A portion of this time is spent playing and the remainder marching. During the winter more time is spent on concert repertoire as the band makes many concert appearances such as the Military Ball and regular concerts. In the spring the band plays all the reviews of the Military Department.

The majority of the larger instruments, such as Basses, Drums, and French Horns, are owned by the University. The band receives its major support from the Athletic Department, Military Department and School of Music. Each year the Athletic Department gives the band a football trip.

Taken from Tales of the Cornhuskers
Nebraska's Athletic Magazine
November 9, 1940

Chapter Four

Game Day Hits The Big Time

Stanford Speed Tops Husker Power in 'Greatest Rose Bowl Tilt,' 21-13

Federal Reserve Asks 'Curbs' on Inflation Danger

Mad Scramble as Motorists Go to Bowl

Nebraska Float Wins Second in Contest

Vike Francis, Zikmund Tally for Nebraskans

It looked as though the Huskers might prevail in their quest to defeat mighty Stanford when Vike Francis burst across the goal line and then converted from placement to put the Huskers out in front 7-0 with just four minutes gone in the game, but the Indians' Little Pete Kmetovic proved too much for the Husker defense and Standford went on to win the contest, 21-13.

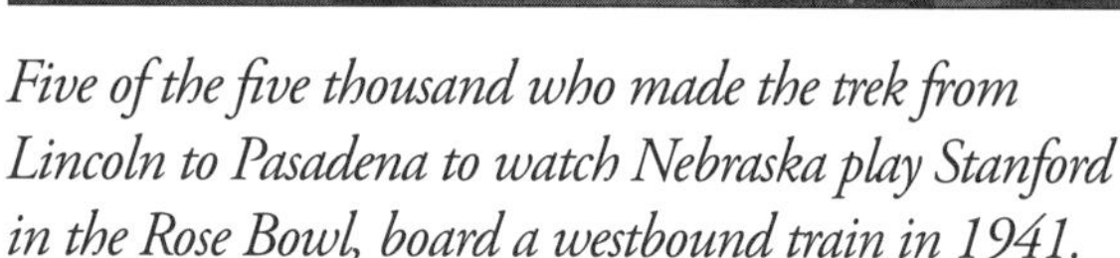

Five of the five thousand who made the trek from Lincoln to Pasadena to watch Nebraska play Stanford in the Rose Bowl, board a westbound train in 1941.

Left: A gorgeous engraved ticket for the Stanford-Nebraska match-up.

Below: Souvenir program from the Annual Tournament of Roses Parade in Pasadena, CA.

Far Left: A patch from the uniform of a member of the University of Nebr. Marching Band in 1941.

Remembering Between the Glory Years

The 1941 Nebraska - Stanford game in the Rose Bowl marked the end of Nebraska's first Glory Years. Toward the end of 1941, Japan attacked Pearl Harbor in Hawaii and we were propelled into World War II. The war years were not kind to College Football. Mobilization for the war took many young men into the military and as a result, College Football took a back seat to the war effort. During those years, our High Schools had football teams and of course, we played football amongst ourselves, so we were able to hold a high interest in the game. At that time, I actually thought some of the High School Football teams were almost as good as some of the College Football teams.

In 1945 when I was in the 6th grade, Don Whitney, my neighbor and fellow 6th grader got hold of a couple of Knothole tickets to a Husker game. I think we paid all of 15 cents or maybe 25 cents (I don't remember which) to sit in the Knothole Section. The Knothole section was made up of bleachers that were setup just beyond the south end zone of the stadium. As I remember, Nebraska played Illinois that day but I could possibly be wrong about that because when I asked Don at our last high school breakfast, he said that we had played Indiana. (Our graduating class from Northeast still meets twice a month for breakfast). Anyway, in spite of what he says, I am still sure it was Illinois.

We paid our 5 cents to ride the bus downtown (yes, bus fare one-way was only 5 cents then) and then walked from "O" Street to the stadium. On our way to the stadium, I remember seeing many uniformed young men. Most were Army but many also were Navy. I also remember seeing a number of temporary buildings set up on the grounds east of Memorial Stadium, located between Morrill Hall to the south and the Coliseum to the north. I assumed these were classrooms and were used to train the many military men that passed through Lincoln during the war. I remember the military being very big on all of the sports at that time. The military academies of course, held the limelight in football all during the war. I remember that Glenn Davis and Doc. Blanchard were the big names in football back then when they played for the Military Academy at West Point. The Army/Navy Game was also a big deal at that time and drew big headlines. Even our own Lincoln Army Air Base had its own very good basketball team called the Lincoln Wings. They had a wonderful basketball player named Goose Tatum, who after war earned fame by playing for the Harlem Globe Trotters. We kids really marveled on how Goose could pick up a basketball with one hand. Later in the 1960's, I took my boys to see him play (it was more of a show built around him than a basketball game) with the Globe Trotters at Pershing Auditorium.

As I remember it, the weather was perfect for football that day, but the field was not in very good shape. It had a lot of brown grass mixed with a bit of green grass in it and it was pretty beat up in the middle of the field. During warm ups, we saw that the Illinois players had black and white uniforms and were really huge compared to our players so I thought it would be a long day for the home team, but I still had hopes that we would win. Our players of course had their Crimson and Cream uniforms and looked a lot neater than their opposition. I believe George Clark was the coach for Nebraska, but I think he was just an interim coach appointed for the 1945 season and that Bernie Masterson had already been selected as the new coach for the 1946 season. I remember being optimistic about the hopes for Nebraska during that next season. I also remember the name of an NU player named Alex Fink who had played High School football for Lincoln High that was on the NU team. I remember seeing him warming up before the game but I'm not sure if he was even able to get into the game that day. As I remember, the players just ran out on to field to play…no tunnel walk or any of that kind of stuff. Anyway, it didn't take long to see that Nebraska was greatly outmanned and to our great disappointment, Illinois just rolled over Nebraska. The most used formation on offense in those days was the "Single Wing" so almost every play was a running play around either end, off tackle or just down the middle. There was very little passing. Also at that time, most of the players still played both offense and defense. I think the idea then was to have their fastest players in the game as much as they could. Therefore, the game by today's standards was pretty boring. By half time, Don and I were less interested in the game and more interested in the crowd and we noticed that most of the uppermost seats in the stadium were empty. Therefore, we slipped out of the Knothole section, snuck up to better seats way up on the west side, and watched the rest of the game from there. I don't remember the final score but I am sure Nebraska lost by a big margin.

Unfortunately, Nebraska was never in national prominence again until 1962, when Bob Devaney came to Nebraska, but there were some spurts of exciting football at NU, like when Tom Novak played 1946-1949 and when Bobby Renolds played in 1950-1952.

Ron Vogel

TURN WAR STAMPS INTO BONDS TO BACK OUR FIGHTING FORCES

OFFICIAL
GAME
PROGRAM

NEBRASKA vs. INDIANA
–Homecoming Day–
OCTOBER 14, 1944

OFFICIAL 25¢ PROGRAM

MINNESOTA vs. NEBRASKA
MEMORIAL STADIUM
OCTOBER 6, 1945

SAFE
RESERVED $3.00
Est. Price $2.50 Fed. Tax 50c
9 24 7 5
SEC. ROW SEAT
INDIANA VS NEBRASKA
SAT., OCTOBER 14, 1944 • 2:00 P. M.
VERSUS
NEBR
SAT.,
2:00 P. M.
MEMORIAL STA

Home and away, the hearts and minds of all Nebraskans were with our men in uniform, stationed overseas and keeping the world safe for democracy. Whether hurling a football or a hand grenade, the images depicted on football programs went a long way toward echoing that sense of national pride that loomed large in stadiums across the country.

Half the Fun is Getting There!

Whether a spartan boxcar or a luxurious lounge, the fun of travelling to an "away" game was definitely in the company you kept. Photo at left depicts the "Football Special", a humbly-appointed boxcar heading to Minnesota that featured ham salad or cheese sandwiches for 20¢, and plenty of Cornhusker spirit. Below: A few years later, these fans looked to enjoying a few more of the creature comforts as this lounge car aptly illustrates. Either way, a good time was had by all.

CODE OF SPORTSMANSHIP

1. I will consider my athletic opponents and the officials as my guest and will treat them as such.
2. I will cheer both teams as they come on the field of play.
3. I will applaud good plays made by either team.
4. I will not applaud errors.
5. I will not "razz" the players of either team or anyone officially connected with either team.
6. I will accept the officials as the proper authorities to make decisions and I will accept their decisions.
7. I will not yell or "razz" during the infliction of a penalty.
8. I will not stir up any unfriendly rivalry among the fans.

The equipment for a football player costs fifty dollars

Chart of the Game

For those who want a graphic account of the game we have prepared 4 grids in order that they may chart the game by quarters. Below are a few conventional signs to be used. The solid black squares represent the first-downs for the oposite team each succeeding square represents a down. Likewise the solid circles and cirlces represent downs for the home team. Remember you chart the ball as it traverses from one end of the field to the other (the yards gained or lost) not as it is carried parallel to the grid lines. The chart shows the progress down the field rather than position on the field.

OPPONENT'S BALL — DROP KICK
NEBRASKA'S BALL — FORWARD PASS
PUNT — PENALTY
RUN — FUMBLE

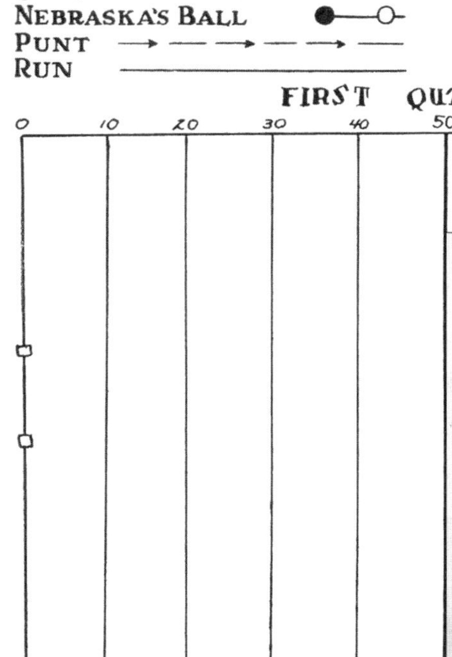

NEBRASKA YELLS

U-U-U-n-i
Ver-ver-ver-si-ti
N-e-bras-ki
Oh-h my!
U-N-Rah-Rah!
U-N-Rah-Rah!
U-Rah—N-Rah!
U-N-Rah-Rah!

3 YEA TEAMS

Yea Team,
Yea Team,
Yea Team,
FIGHT!
FIGHT!
FIGHT!

He's-a-man,
Whose a man,
He's a NEBRASKA MAN

LOCOMOTIVE YELL
Rah! Rah! Rah! Rah! Nebras-ka!
Nebras-ka!
Rah! Rah! Rah! Rah! Nebras-ka!
Nebras-ka!
Rah! Rah! Rah! Rah! Nebras-ka!
Nebras-ka!
Hoo-Rah! Nebras-ka! ! !

Nebraska Songs

"THE CORNHUSKER"

Come a-runnin', boys,
Don't you hear that noise
Like the thunder in the skies,
How it rolls along
In the good old song,
For the sons of Nebraski.
Now it's coming near
With a rising cheer
That will sweep all foes away,
So, with all our vim,
We are bound to win,
And we're going to win today—

CHORUS

For Nebraska and the Scarlet,
For Nebraska and the Cream
Tho they go through many a battle
Our colors still are seen.
So in contest and in victory
We will wave them for the team
And 'twill always stir a Cornhusker
The Old Scarlet and the Cream.

CHANT

U-Rah, N-Rah,
U-N-I-
U-Varsity, N-Varsity,
Ne-bras-ki,
Ne-bras-ki.

There is no place like Nebraska,
Dear old Nebraska U,
Where the girls are the fairest,
The boys are the squarest
Of any old place that you know.
There is no place like Nebraska,
Where they're all true blue,
We'll all stick together,
In all kinds of weather,
For dear old Nebraska U.

Page Twenty *Tales of the Cornhuskers*

FOOTBALL GLOSSARY
Officiating, Coaching and Playing Terms

By John W. Heisman

Angle Play: Runner heads for boundary then cuts at right angles into line.
Backer-Up: Middle player in secondary defensive line.
Backs: The men who play in the offensive backfield.
Backfield: The four offensive players behind the rush line.
Ball: Circum: 28 in. by 22½ in. Weight 14-15 oz.
Battting the Ball: Forward batting illegal save on forward passes.
Blocking: Interference—checking of tacklers by offensive players.
Bowl Defense: Rushline surrounding offense in bowl-like corral.
Box Defense: Seven on rush line, two in secondary and two in territory.
Boxing the Tackle: Outflanking defensive tackle, turning him IN.
Changing Goals: Teams must, after first and third periods.
Change of Pace: Runner's purposeful change of running speeds.
Charging: Going into action on snapping the ball.
Cleats: Anti-slipping, leather strips on the soles of player's shoes.
Clipping: Diving into defensive player's legs from behind. Illegal.
Close Formation: Offense. No back more than 6 yards back of line.
Completed Forward Pass: One caught legally by eligible receiver.
Crawling: Tackled runner advancing ball when down. Illegal.
Crest: Longitudinal ridge or middle of field—from goal to goal.
Criss-Cross: Old name for double-pass around end. The "Reverse" play.
Cross-Bar: Is 10 ft. above ground. Field goal must go over.
Cutback: **Offense.** Runner starts toward end then sharply cuts back and through.
Cycle (of Plays): Offense. A number of plays starting alike but working out differently.
Dead Ball: During enforcement of penalties and when "Time" has been called. Not in play.
Delayed Buck: A fake buck aimed at one spot followed by real buck hitting elsewhere.
Delaying the Game: Slow signalling or lining-up to kill time.
Diamond Defense: Seven on line, one in secondary, two halves in tertiary line, "safety" man far back.
Direct Snap: Runner gets ball directly from the snapper-back.
Disqualification: A penalty—player is removed from game.
Double-Pass: Offense. Player first getting ball passes it to another.
Double-Teaming: Two offense players combining on one defensive man.
Down: Occurs when referee blows whistle or declares ball dead.
Drop-Kick: Dropping ball and kicking it on the rebound.
Eligible: Offensive player having right to catch a forward pass.
End: The player on either extremity of the rush line.
End Line: Back line of the end zone, on which goal posts are placed.
End Run: Offense. A "sweep" play aimed at the defensive extremity.
End Zone: The 10-yards-wide rectangle beyond either goal line.
Equipment: Must be safe—no nails or projectting metal.
Fair Catch: Catching a punt after raising the arm. No run or tackle allowed after such signal and catch.
Fake Play: Offense. Giving a false indication of kind of play.
False Start: Any fake move calculated to draw defense offside. Illegal.
Feint to Snap: Preliminary false moving of the ball. Illegal.
Field Goal: Drop or Place Kick over the bar not following touchdown.
Field Judge: The official who mainly watches forward pass plays.
Field of Play: 300 ft. long, 160 ft. wide. (Exclusive of end zones).
Flat Pass: A forward pass toward side line—only slightly forward.
Forfeited Game: 1-0 against—when team refuses to accept ruling.
Formation: Offense. Arrangement of linemen and backs for a play.
Forward: One who plays on the rush line.
Forward Pass: Legal under conditions of Rule 7, Sec. 5.
Forward Progress: of Runner Stopped: Down is ended ball is "dead."
Foul: Any violation of a rule.
Free Kick: Any kick where defensive team must stand 10 yds. from ball.
Full Back: The offensive back who does most of the line bucking.
Fumble: Dropping of the ball by the player carrying or catching it.
Game: Consists of four quarters or Periods of 15 min. each.
Goal From Field: Same as Field Goal.
Goal Line: Between the Field of Play and the End Zone.
Goal Posts: Must be 20 ft. high and 18 ft. 6 in. apart. On End Line.
Guard: The player next to, and on either side of, the snapper-back.
Head Linesman: Official who assists the referee.
Helping or **"Hiking"** the Runner, by pulling, pushing, lifting. Illegal.
Hidden Ball: Offense. Deceiving defense as to which back has the ball by "faking" to give it to various backs.
Hole: The runner's objective spot in the rush line.
Huddle: Offense. Players group compactly to get their signal.
Hurdling: Runner jumping over defensive line with both feet foremost. Illegal.
(Continued in Iowa Issue of Tales of Cornhuskers)

Dreams In Scarlet & Cream

By Mary Jane Nielsen & Jon Roth

It's every Dad's dream
to help raise a Husker;
Through the years it will take
All the strength he can muster.

He'll patiently wait
for his tyke to grow up;
As the boy learns to play
like a pro, not a pup.

His pageants, his glory,
the fans on the field,
Are the junk and the plants
that a sandlot might yield.

But, he'll soon reach the field,
Time to sleep and to dream,
Of the time when he plays
for the Scarlet & Cream.

Come on down town after the game and enjoy the Cornhusker's famous "Football Buffet"—it's "SCHIMMEL service" at its finest! Heap your plate with tempting hors d'oerves and entrees, including succulent roast prime rib of beef and tender Baked Lancaster ham. You're always welcome at the Cornhusker—no reservations needed.

in the GEORGIAN ROOM
serving 5:30 - 8:30 p. m.

Specify "SCHIMMELservice" for certified comfort, courtesy and cuisine in these other great midwestern cities . . .

Next football Saturday, meet at the Cornhusker's Football Buffet Luncheon, serving from 11 a.m. 'til game time in the Georgian Room.

HOTEL CORNHUSKER
13th & M
A. Q. Schimmel, Managing Director

. . . and in Omaha, it's the BLACKSTONE HOTEL, home of the Cottonwood Room, the Plush Horse, and the gracious Orleans Room.

HOTEL LASSEN
Wichita, Kansas

The TOWN HOUSE
Kansas City, Kansas

HOTEL CUSTER
Galesburg, Illinois

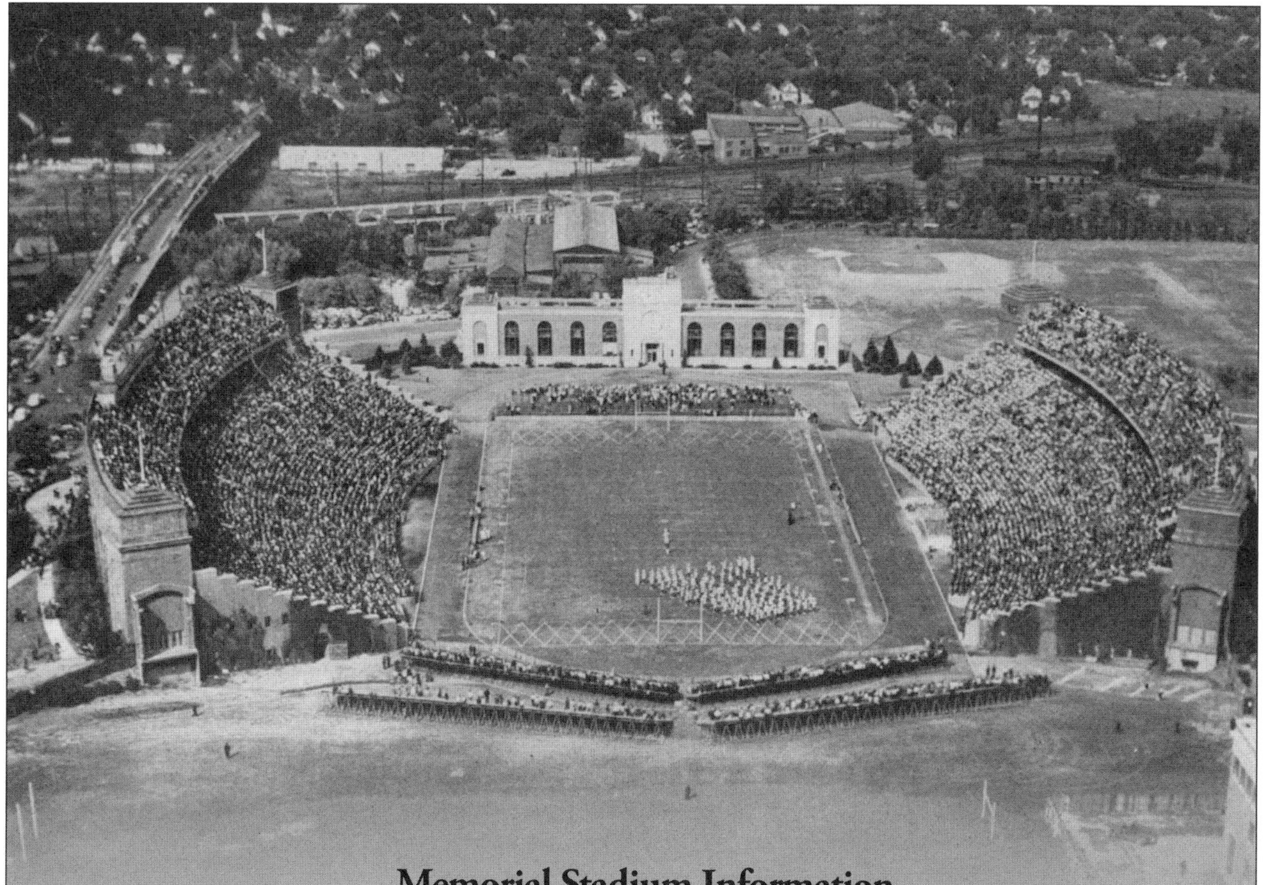

Memorial Stadium Information

Lost & Found Articles Lost articles should be reported to Lost and Found Dept., West Stadium. Those finding articles should turn them in at same place. Persons who have lost articles may learn whether or not the property has been turned in by telephoning 2-7631, extension 3246, on Monday following the date of the game.

First Aid Emergency treatment is available in the trainer's room, Field House, located at the north end of the playing field.

Announcements Over Public Address System No announcements under any circumstance are made over the public address system. If you are expecting calls during the game, leave your seat number and name with the ticket takers. Ushers will notify you if the calls materialize.

Rest Rooms Women's rest rooms are located at the north end of the concourse in both east and west stadiums. Men's rest rooms are at the south end of each stadium.

Telephones Public pay stations are located in both the east and west stadiums.

"...Man, Woman

"It was a time of open communication and great camaraderie."

–Gil Savery

As you have read in other pages in this book, you know Nebraska football fans have always had a great time partying and tailgating before and after games – both home and away. Behind the scenes, other things emerged as a byproduct of gridiron news coverage.

Decades ago, sports editors, reporters and photographers accompanied Cornhusker coaches and players as they traveled by rail to away games. It was a time of open communication and great camaraderie.

While sports staffers of the Lincoln newspapers, focused on football more than other sports, they built reputations that catapulted them to sports-related careers.

and Child...!"

Often they ended up in other cities, but not Charles Sumner "Cy" Sherman. Before he became sports editor of the Lincoln Star, Cy was a sports writer for the Nebraska State Journal. It was during that time that he called the Nebraska football team the Cornhuskers. Later it became the official name. That made Cy famous right here in Lincoln where Notre Dame's Four Horsemen were defeated. Later Bob Devaney and Tom Osborne were to coach five national championship teams.

Long ago there was no such position at Nebraska as Sports Information Director (SID). Waiting in the wings, however, was one John Bentley, sports editor of the Journal and briefly its city editor. John left the Journal to write for the Omaha World-Herald. He returned to Lincoln and became the University of Nebraska's first sports information director.

Later Don "Fox" Bryant, a Lincoln Star sports editor, became SID and brought a ready smile, winsome personality and abundant talent and knowledge to the job, which spanned three decades. No one knows more about Cornhusker football, and all Husker sports, than Don. He had been the Star's sports editor for 10 years.

Don's long resume includes his serving two active tours of duty with the U.S. Marine Corps, and being involved with the winter Olympics in 1980, 1984 and 1988. His awards in the sports field are extensive. He was inducted into the Nebraska Journalism Hall of Fame, jointly awarded by the Nebraska Press Association and the University of Nebraska-Lincoln's College of Journalism and Mass Communication. He is also the recipient the Nebraskaland Foundation's Wagonmaster Award.

Dick Becker, a longtime Lincoln Journal sports editor, became general manager of Ak-Sar-Ben. That was back when that organization was thriving and its major activities included horse racing, stock shows, and prime entertainment. Dick had a great knowledge of sports and a good business head – knowing how to delegate work and seeing that goals were achieved.

Virgil Parker, a onetime announcer and owner of an Oregon radio station, successfully shifted to print journalism and became sports editor of the Lincoln Journal Star. He was a great storyteller. When Parker left the newspaper, he became head of the Nebraska Golf Association where he applied his journalistic and managerial skills to a sport that was rapidly becoming more popular.

Quite a number of well-known sports writers who were not editors left newspaper reporting for other careers, some related to sports and others not. Quickly coming to mind are Wally Provost, who worked for the Lincoln Journal and later developed a large audience when writing sports columns for the Omaha World-Herald.

Mike Babcock took the buyout offered staff members when Lee Enterprises bought the Seacrest family interest in the Journal-Star Printing Company. Cornhusker football fans are well acquainted with his splendid and successful career in freelance reporting.

Randy York, who left Lincoln sports writing for a position with Sprint in Kansas City, returned to Lincoln and is now an assistant athletic director under Tom Osborne. He is known to fans through his popular Randy York's Nsider report. It was Randy who first introduced me to Coach Osborne at a Cornhusker practice. Osborne would have no reason to remember me, but we have a few things in common. Both have wives from Holdrege. Both have taught United Methodist Sunday school, both have been church lay leaders, and both have had the same heart surgeon repair our ailing hearts. Osborne had his surgery before I had mine. Our seats were about 30 rows up behind the Nebraska bench. Seeing him jog onto the field in Memorial Stadium boosted my morale only a month or two after my surgery.

Fingers that touched typewriter and computer keyboards recording Cornhusker football action also opened wide the doors to other careers – mostly sports-related.

All this was happening as Cornhusker fans were flocking to Memorial Stadium, tuning their radios, reading newspapers for pre-game insights or making sure they were in just the right spot to catch on TV every play made by their beloved Cornhuskers.

Husker football glues Nebraskans together – north to south and east to west -- as no other activity or interest. We hope that holds true as our Huskers join the Big Ten Conference.

The historic Husker shift will not be the first penetration of the Big Ten by Nebraska. Herman Rohrig, Lincoln High School star athlete and a University of Nebraska Football Hall of Fame inductee, became head of Big Ten officiating. He was a 1936 LHS graduate along with other notable athletes and coaches such as William "Bill" Pfeiff, a Nebraska High School Sports Hall of Fame inductee. We were classmates at Lincoln High and the University.

Football writers and editors career changes were indeed often launched by Cornhusker football. As Dick Cavett often reminds us: There Is No Place Like Nebraska!

Gil Savery

Chapter Five

Game Day Gets Televised

Nebraska Football

My memories of Nebraska football start at the age of 6 or 7, which takes us to the 40s. Nebraska always played Oklahoma on Thanksgiving Day. My father worked at the Lincoln Telephone and Telegraph Company and was the trouble shooter in the Press Box at the stadium. Mother would get very upset because Dad was working on Thanksgiving Day and missed the big dinner.

As soon as I was old enough, I bought a knothole ticket. These were sold in the Public Schools and it allowed you to go to the home games for a dime or 25 cents.

I would leave my house on 33rd and "R", walk to Vine Street and along the way meet friends, each of us carrying a bag of home popped popcorn and an apple. We would walk to the Stadium and sit in the bleachers on the north end of the stadium – We would cheer and the cheerleaders would come to our section and get us to cheer louder. After the game we walked back home and usually stopped at 27th & Vine and would buy something to either eat or drink at Gus's Market or Wagey Drug soda fountain.

In high school, I worked at Gold's on Saturdays and one of my jobs was to pass out red feathers with an "N" on them. It seemed like everybody wanted a red feather.

I married and moved to Colorado and later to Missouri, but we always tried to get back to Nebraska games. While in Missouri, we bought season tickets and each year friends from Lincoln would come to Missouri for the game. The weekends were always great times.

My son now has Missouri season tickets and we still go back and forth on the weekends when Missouri plays Nebraska.

This year will end a tradition that started 50 years ago with Missouri people coming to Lincoln for the big football weekend. Nebraska is a great place to play football and they have fantastic fans. These memories will last forever.

Sandy Hergert

My Trip to Notre Dame vs. Nebraska · October 18, 1947

I had a season ticket to games in Nebraska at least one or two years, especially 1947.

Midway thru 1947 (May, I believe) I was released from service duty, being stationed at Fort Meyer, Virginia, and working at the Pentagon. When I got home to Nebraska, I purchased a season ticket to Nebraska football games. I had started working at the CB&Q railroad helping clean train coaches. One benefit was being able to ride the train free.

I was a fan of Johnny Lujack, Quarterback for Notre Dame, so I decided to attend the game. I rode the train to Chicago and then took a bus to South bend to the stadium. I saved the program, plus a picture of Johnny Lujack and three football trinkets.

This was quite an experience for a farmboy at heart and a mere 20 years of age. The highlights of my trip were seeing Nebraska play Notre Dame, and then while in Chicago, I was able to attend the Roy Rogers Rodeo. Roy was my movie hero.

My season ticket was on the West side in the first balcony, first row. Why did I ever quit purchasing it?

Jack Schubert

Football Tickets

When I started working for Latsch Brothers, Inc. in 1946, one of the first tasks was to place the 10 foot tall football player sign on the front marquee at 1124 "O" Street. The cabinet shop made the sign with a wood frame faced on both sides with masonite, painted in Nebraska Scarlett & Cream.

Latsch's sold both general admission and reserve seat tickets during home game week. During the week, we sold a few tickets, but on Saturday, if it was a nice day, people would be lined up outside the front door to buy tickets. When we opened at 9:00 am, we lined them up on the west isle and out on the east isle. We sold them until 1964, after Bob Devaney's second year. After that, pre-sales were at the ticket office (inside the front door of the Coliseum, managed by A. J. Lewandowski). This was the beginning of the "sell-outs".

In John Sellick's memoirs, John made mention that the Sellecks and Jerome Latsch played bridge. One night John (Athletic Business Manager) complained about not having enough money to start the football season. J. E. asked him if he ever thought of selling "Season Tickets". John asked, "what do you mean?". J. E. replied, what about stapling all of the tickets for each reserve seat section ahead of the season. John asked if J .E. thought they would sell? J. E. Latsch answered, "I'll buy two and my brother will buy two". John tried it and it was a success. Through the years the University asked businesses to buy more "Season tickets" and many of them bought blocks of tickets.

Herbert G. Henry

A Fine, Feathered Trend that Featured an "N"

I wish I could be more specific on dates, but during 1945-1960 at Gold & Co. Department Store in downtown Lincoln, they gave away Red "N" Feathers on game days. I know this because my husband Dwayne "Goldie" Goldsmith, an employee there at the time, was one of those dispensing feathers to customers entering through the north doors around 1947-1951. The feathers were around 8" long and red with a white glossy paper N on the top…

He also remembers the Knot-Hole Section where "kids" could get into the UNL football games for 25 cents – the boys sat on bleachers in the south end of the stadium and the girls on the north! Because of the war, they were allowed to sit high up in the west stadium, because the seats were not full…

Sometime during the 1947-1951 span, Dwayne's College View High School coach, Tom Gillespie was in charge of setting up and taking care of personnel in the Press Box. Dwayne remembers helping by carrying typewriters up there, putting a program at each individual place and, delivering any food requested (mostly hotdogs). For doing this, he got into the game for free.

He also remembers later helping to paint the benches in the south stadium!

We are 77 and 75, respectfully now and remember many wonderful away games including Hawaii, and all the great times we have had as long-time season ticket holders. Back when the snow was deep and women in the east and west stadiums wore fur coats! Once we parked behind the stadium and when we came out the car was gone. The police had hauled it way down by the Court House; so we just parked there the rest of the year!

My husband remembers favorite coaches Bo Pelini, Tom Osborne, Bob Devaney and "Potsy" Clark.

Mr. & Mrs. Dwayne "Goldie" Goldsmith

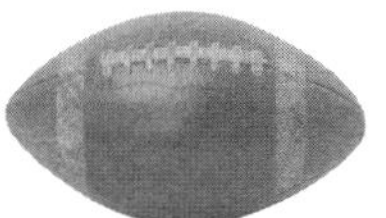

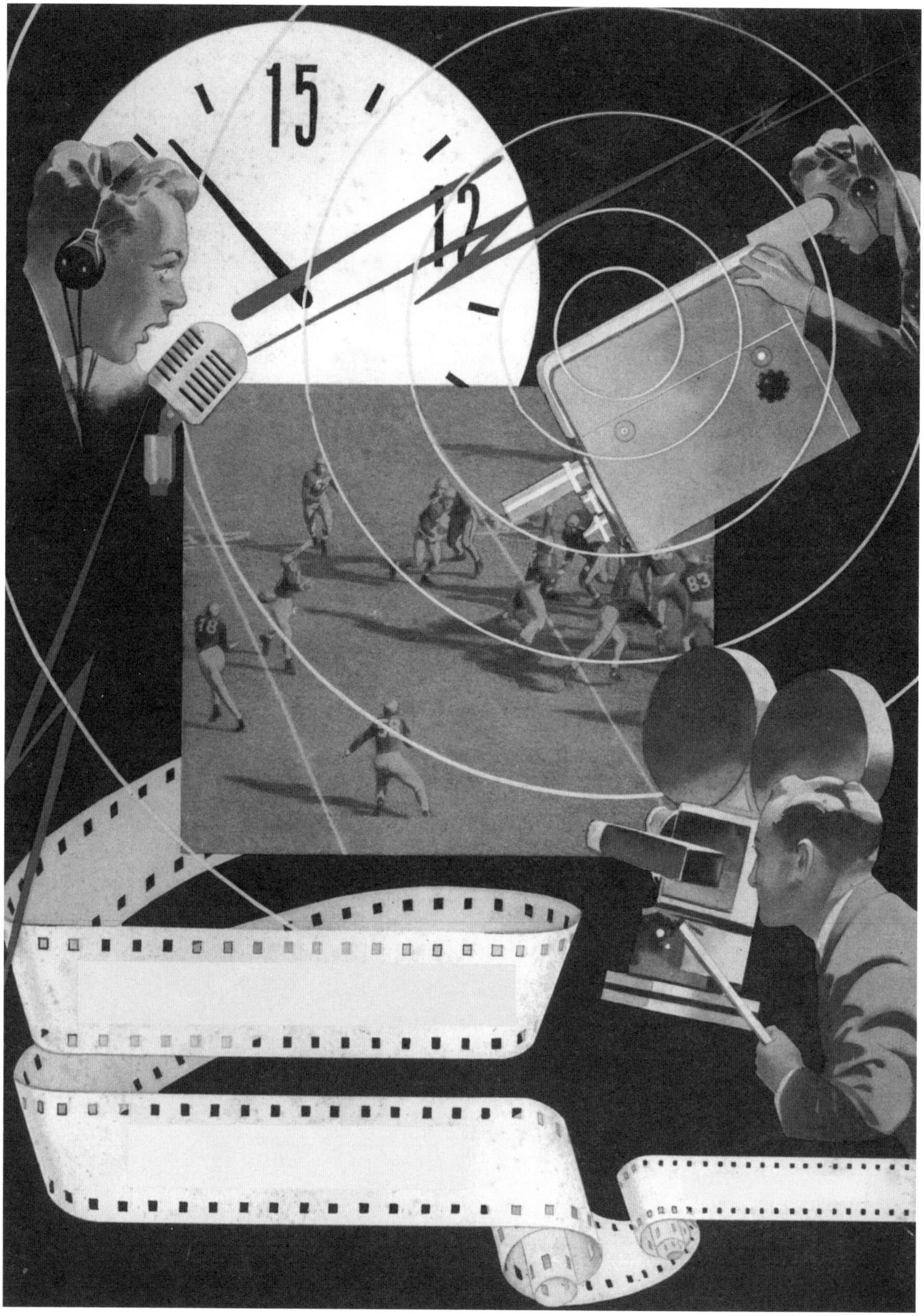

Sending Out All The Right Signals

When I was in College View High School, I would go to a Nebraska game at Memorial Stadium. I would sit in the bleachers in the south end zone. My ticket was called a "knothole ticket" and the cost was twenty five cents. A real bargain!

The Stadium seated 38,000 and was never sold out. In addition to the tickets sold each week by the University Ticket Office, tickets were sold every Saturday morning before the game at all of the banks and utility offices downtown.

Many years later while I was working for Lincoln Telephone and Telegraph Company, we were asked if we could install equipment to televise a home football game. I installed that equipment for the first televised game and continued to do that through the years for the other games that were selected to be televised.

In later years, I was placed in charge of the crew who made all this possible. We used Microwave Radio to send the signal to the national networks: ABC, CBS, NBC and ESPN.

I became familiar with the players and the changes every year. I even followed their achievements in their professional careers.

Today on home game Saturdays before the game begins, parking lots in downtown Lincoln become a "party zone". During the game there are very few vehicles driving in downtown Lincoln. When a great play is made on the field, you can hear the ROAR all over downtown Lincoln.

Cornhusker football has been an important part of my life. Go Big Red!

Wallace Gake

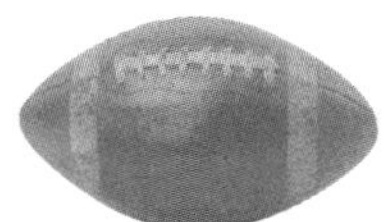

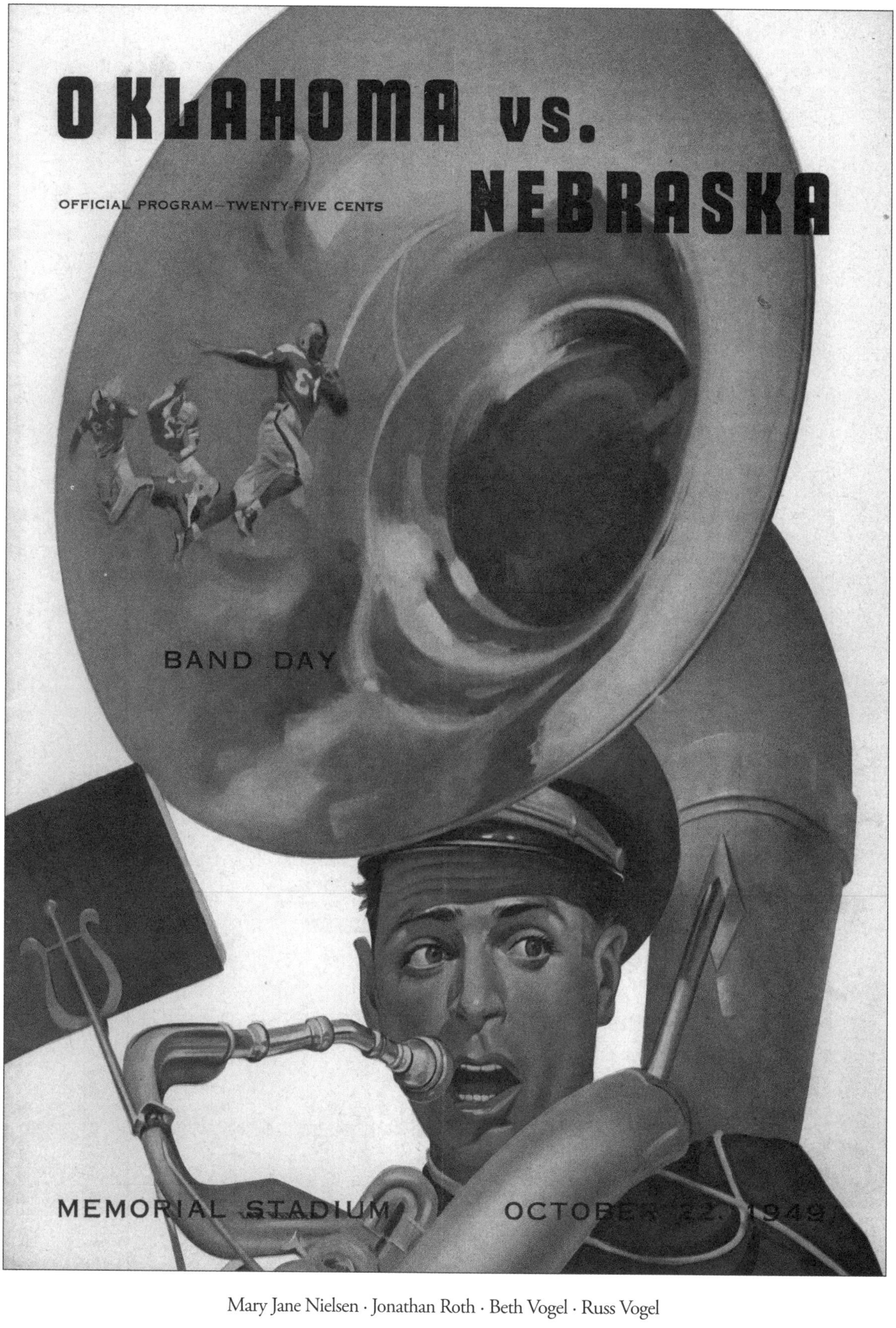

OKLAHOMA vs. NEBRASKA

OFFICIAL PROGRAM—TWENTY-FIVE CENTS

BAND DAY

MEMORIAL STADIUM OCTOBER 22, 1949

Half-Time Entertainment

The University of Kansas band will help the University of Nebraska and its great 120-piece marching band celebrate Homecoming Day.

The Jayhawks, under the direction of Mr. Russell Wiley, will perform the intial six minutes of the half-time period.

The Nebraska band, conducted by Prof. Donald Lentz, will then take the field. The Huskers will do a precision drill based on cart-wheels with alternating pivots. The band will form an "N", featuring the entire trumpet section in a specialty, "The Three Jacks" by Waters. As a finale, Homecoming Queen Mary Helen Mallory, of Lincoln, will be presented to the crowd. The band will make an outline of the State of Nebraska, enclosing a heart of Tassels and Corn Cobs, women's and men's pep organizations.

The presentation of Miss Mallory will be made by Nebraska Chancellor R. G. Gustavson.

The student card section will accompany the mottoes on the field with the following stunts. (1) A salute to Kansas. (2) A salute to the Big Seven Conference. (3) A Homecoming tribute to all old grads. (4) A mirror of the band's Homecoming queen formation.

OFFICIAL PROGRAM—TWENTY-FIVE CENTS

U. C. L. A.

VS.

NEBRASKA

HOMECOMING

MEMORIAL STADIUM

OCTOBER 30, 1948

Nebraska
If in this color you believe,
Then put this emblem on your sleeve

Location. Location. Location.

Immanuel Church is the little white Church at the bottom of the overpass by Memorial Stadium. For years the ladies of our church would bake Runzas to sell on game day. The line of people to get into the fellowship hall would sometimes go for nearly a block with dozens of people already inside enjoying their hot, homemade Runzas. People would call ahead to order one, two or twenty Runzas and each week the ladies would make nearly 2000 of these kraut sandwiches with a waiting list for any extras.

People were not much different years ago when I was a kid. They loved Runzas just like people do today. However, when I was a kid I remember a time when I wasn't quite as excited about selling them as I have been in recent years at my church.

I recall one Saturday morning that my mother had made Runzas (which were the BEST kraut sandwiches you ever ate) and asked that I take the sandwiches to the stadium to sell before the game. Being a young girl in Junior High I shuddered at the thought of doing this. Have you ever been in a situation like this? The Runzas smelled so good; they were nice and warm, they were a work of art and all I could do was stand and studder "you, you, you really don't want me to do that do you? What if I see some of the girls from school?"

My heart was racing a mile a minute, but being Katherine's obedient child I told Mama that I would do it. I went over to 10th street and held my box of treasures, standing on the edge of the sidewalk, looking in the opposite direction of the stadium. I was aware of people walking behind me and I heard an occasional "Hi Vem" and I would wave. I pretended that I was going somewhere.

Finally I did go home and Mama smiled and said "Did you sell anything? "No Mama, I guess I'm just not good at selling." No one ever saw my wares. To this day I hurt a little when I think of this story because there was not one who was as kind and giving as my Mama and no one could ever make a Runza like she did.

Today, I would proudly sell those Runzas – and no doubt my customers would greatly enjoy them.

That very corner would be where our church would eventually sell-out of Runzas every Football Saturday.

Vemmy Nielsen

Runza Sandwiches

2 medium sized cabbage heads
½ cup vegetable oil
2 lb hamburger
1 cup water
2 medium onions (chopped fine)

Salt & Pepper to taste

Chop cabbage and onion. Add water, oil, salt and pepper. Start cooking on low heat. Brown hamburger. Add to cabbage mixture. Cook until cabbage is done, then strain well. This makes filling for about 24 Runzas.

Runza Dough Put ½ cup lukewarm water in small bowl and add 1 tsp sugar. Sprinkle 1 package dry yeast, let stand for 1 minute. In large bowl, combine 2 cups hot water and 1 stick oleo. Let melt, then add 1 cup milk, ½ cup sugar, 2 tsp salt. Stir until mixture is lukewarm. Add 2 beaten eggs and 3 cups flour. Add yeast mixture in smaller bowl and mix well. Add more flour (until dough is stiff, 6 to 8 cups). Knead well and let rise, punch down and let rise again until double in size. Roll out and make runzas or cinnamon rolls. Bake at 375 degrees until brown.

Or! Use boxed hot roll mix!

It IS Contagious. And, There's Simply No Known Cure.

Question: What say you? What would cause you to stand up and be counted? What would cause you to stand and start shouting and cheering? What is it actually that lights your light? Turns your key? Sparks your hot button? Enough! I just wish I were on the receiving end of the line receiving all the answers that any of these questions might generate from the reader. I would really like to know.

Living in Nebraska, I would chance a guess that our Number One answer to all of the above, would probably be the 'CORNHUSKERS!" They will be coming back soon and that will cause many of us to stand and cheer and shout. In Nebraska, I believe that most of the people do have Cornhusker fever. I don't think there is anyone in Nebraska who loves the HUSKERS more than I do, nor suffers from the fever more than I do. I even have withdrawal pangs when the last game has been played. I always wish for a Bowl Game....so we can anticipate and lessen the agony of future days without them. I also admit that I am a sore loser, but that will be to be a story for another time. Our Huskers are winners even when they lose.

How did this illness get into my bloodstream? It may be hereditary, but I believe it actually came to me as a result of having six brothers. Yes, I said SIX BROTHERS and they each had at least six closed friends and they all loved to replay everyone of the Husker games-not missing a single toss or fumble. I believe we would be fair in calling them "Monday Morning Quarterbacks."

As a very young girl...probably about 8 or 9 years old, my oldest brother Jake asked me if I would like to go to a rally at the University. It was Friday night and I had a piano lesson at the same time. Jake got me excused from the piano lesson and I went with him and a couple of his buddies to the rally. To this day, I claim this to be one of the most outstanding times of my life. The Cheerleaders, the bon fire, the stand that was built on the grounds and the crowd of people, music and my brother making sure that I was able to see everything. What other young girl got to go with her brother and his friends (I don't know that the friends were too happy, but oh well). I had the time of my life.

I do believe I had the fever before that great time, but now I believe I did become addicted to those Huskers and their talents that night. Regarding the piano lessons, I do and can play for my own entertainment. Regarding the addiction which I have for the Huskers, I don't' think I will ever stop cheering for our team nor do I ever want to stop.

By the way, Donald, my high school sweetheart has the Husker Fever as bad as I do. I don't know if I caught it from Donald or if he caught it from me. I do believe he too, is addicted.

GO BIG RED! FIGHT HUSKERS!

Vemmy Nielsen

A television ad for a Sylvania TV touts it as a "Cabinet of Light", but for diehard football fans it might well have been considered a cabinet of life. By the mid 1950s, color television made the scene. The RCA television featured in a Gold's display window at that time, cost a "mere" $750.00.

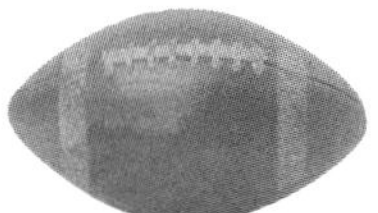

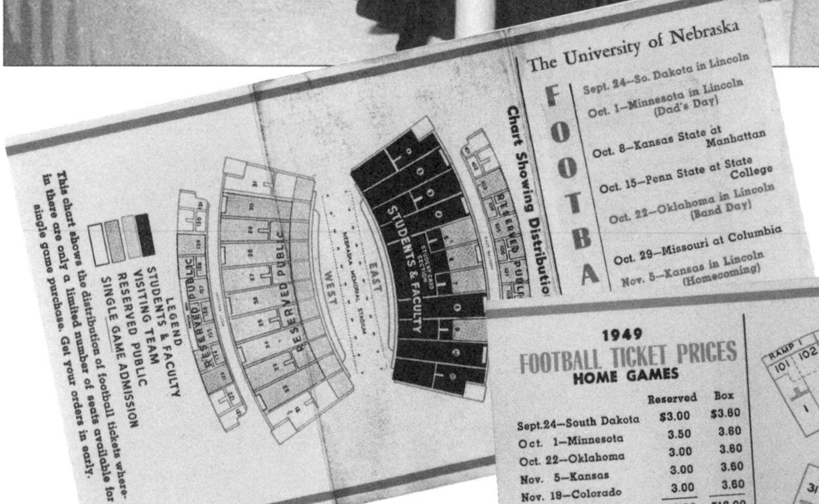

The University of Nebraska

FOOTBA

Sept. 24—So. Dakota in Lincoln
Oct. 1—Minnesota in Lincoln (Dad's Day)
Oct. 8—Kansas State at Manhattan
Oct. 15—Penn State at State College
Oct. 22—Oklahoma in Lincoln (Band Day)
Oct. 29—Missouri at Columbia
Nov. 5—Kansas in Lincoln (Homecoming)

Chart Showing Distributio

RESERVED PUBLIC
STUDENTS & FACULTY
EAST
WEST
RESERVED PUBLIC
RESERVED PUBLIC

LEGEND
STUDENTS & FACULTY
VISITING TEAM
RESERVED PUBLIC
SINGLE GAME ADMISSION

This chart shows the distribution of football tickets wherein there are only a limited number of seats available for single game purchase. Get your orders in early.

1949
FOOTBALL TICKET PRICES
HOME GAMES

	Reserved	Box
Sept.24—South Dakota	$3.00	$3.60
Oct. 1—Minnesota	3.50	3.60
Oct. 22—Oklahoma	3.00	3.60
Nov. 5—Kansas	3.00	3.60
Nov. 19—Colorado	3.00	3.60
SEASON	$15.50	$18.00

All prices above include Tax.
Games start 2 p. m.
Include 25c for all mail orders.

UNIVERSITY
FOOTBALL TICKET OFFICE
Telephone 2-7631
COLISEUM
LINCOLN, NEBRASKA

RAMP 1 · RAMP 3 · RAMPS 5-7 · RAMP 9 · RAMP 11
101 102 103 104 105 106 107 108 109 110 111
1 2 3 4 5 6 7 8 9 10 11
EAST STADIUM
WEST STADIUM
31 30 29 28 27 26 25 24 23 22 21
131 130 129 128 127 126 125 124 123 122 121
PRESS BOX
RAMPS 31 29 27 25 · RAMP 23 · RAMP 21

NEBRASKA
MEMORIAL
STADIUM

NOTE:
The sections and ramps of the Stadium have been re-numbered for your convenience. Be sure to locate your ramp and then section to avoid confusion. Season-ticket holders from previous years will receive the same location even though the ramp and section will be a different number.

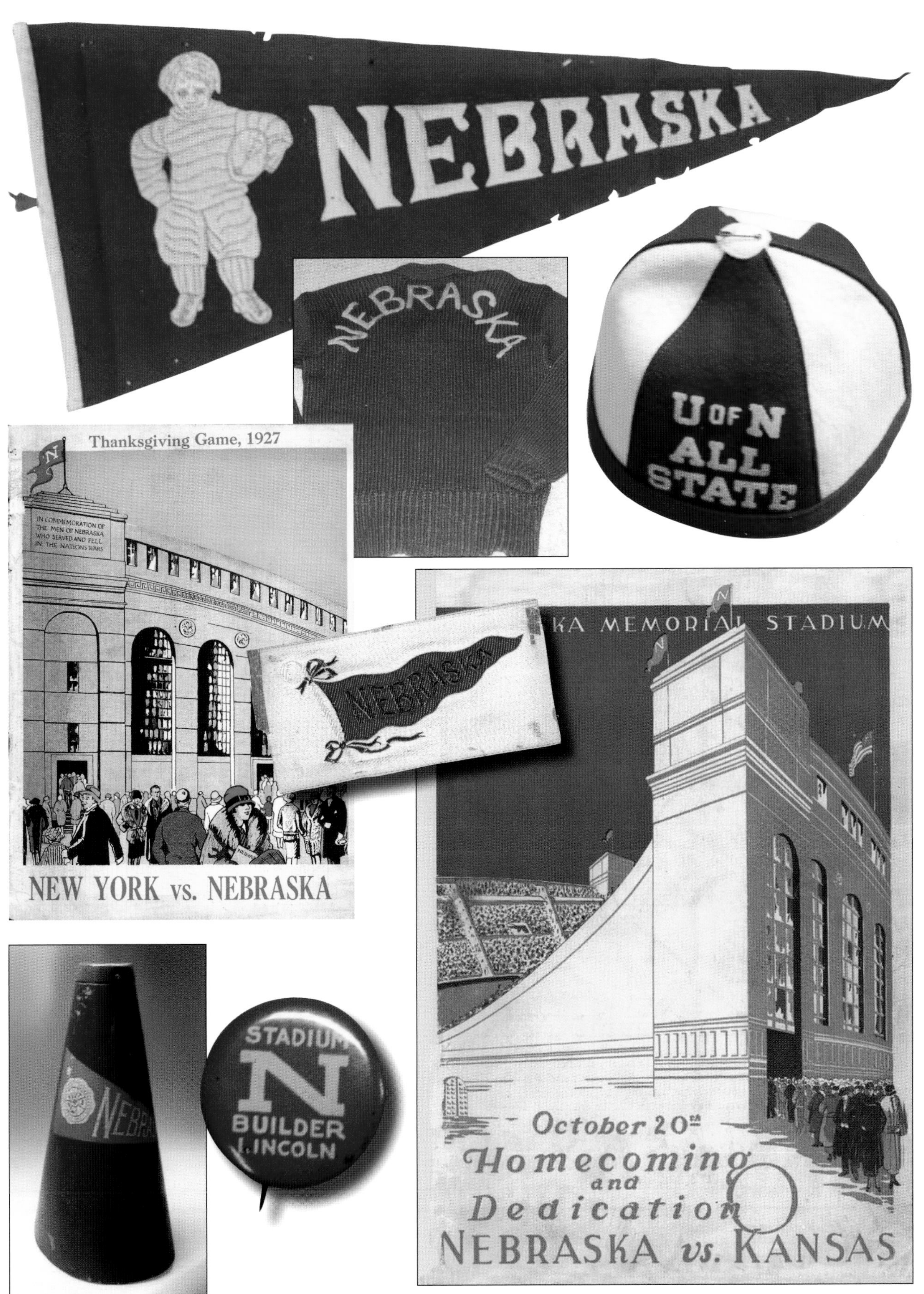
NEBRASKA
NEBRASKA
U OF N
ALL
STATE
Thanksgiving Game, 1927
IN COMMEMORATION OF
THE MEN OF NEBRASKA
WHO SERVED AND FELL
IN THE NATIONS WARS
NEW YORK vs. NEBRASKA
NEBRASKA
KA MEMORIAL STADIUM
October 20th
Homecoming
and
Dedication
NEBRASKA vs. KANSAS
STADIUM
N
BUILDER
LINCOLN
NEBRAS

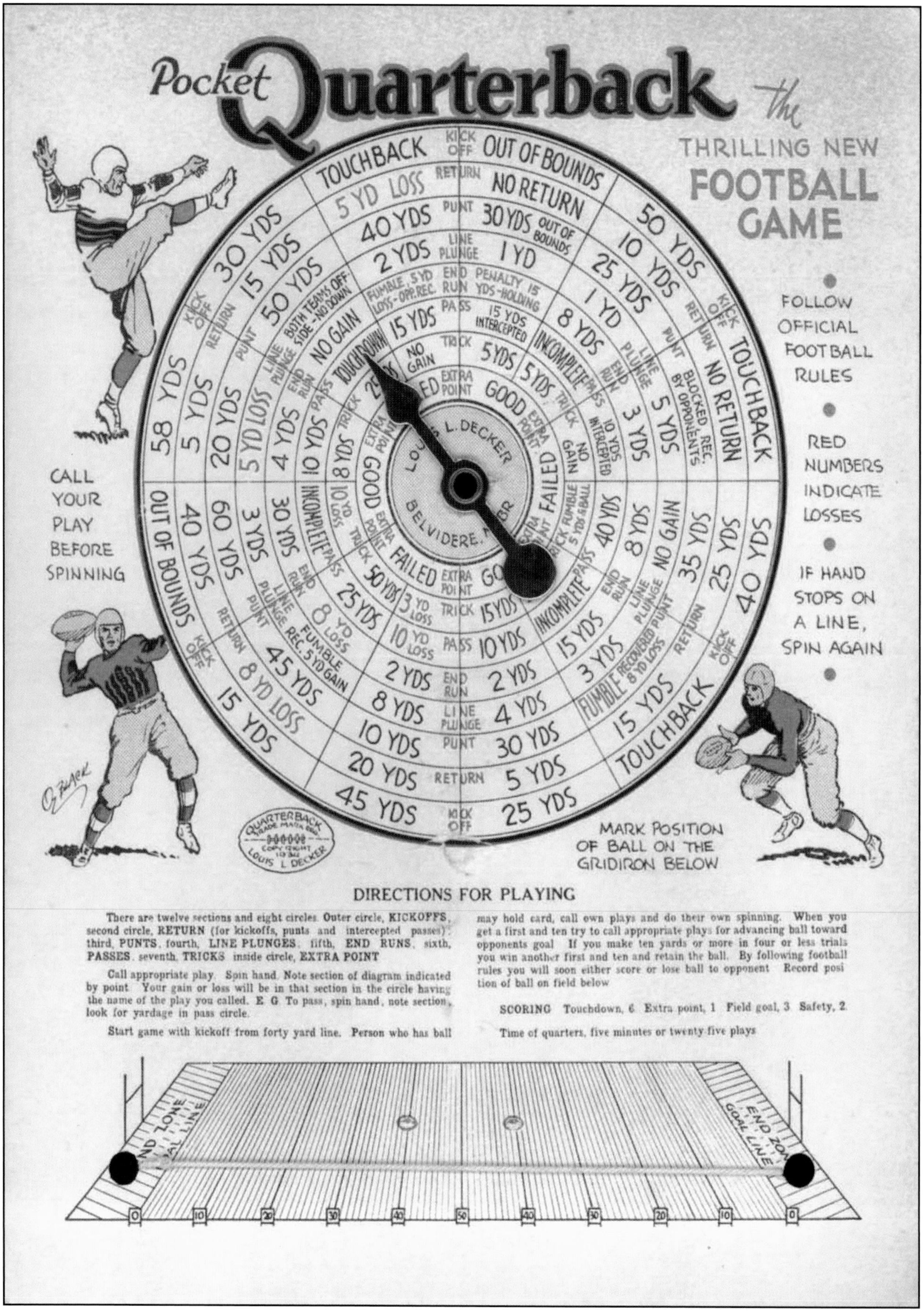

Pocket Quarterback

the THRILLING NEW FOOTBALL GAME

- FOLLOW OFFICIAL FOOTBALL RULES
- RED NUMBERS INDICATE LOSSES
- IF HAND STOPS ON A LINE, SPIN AGAIN

CALL YOUR PLAY BEFORE SPINNING

LOUIS L. DECKER BELVIDERE, NEBR

QUARTERBACK TRADE MARK REG. COPYRIGHT 1934 LOUIS L. DECKER

MARK POSITION OF BALL ON THE GRIDIRON BELOW

DIRECTIONS FOR PLAYING

There are twelve sections and eight circles. Outer circle, **KICKOFFS**, second circle, **RETURN** (for kickoffs, punts and intercepted passes): third, **PUNTS**, fourth, **LINE PLUNGES**, fifth, **END RUNS**, sixth, **PASSES**, seventh, **TRICKS** inside circle, **EXTRA POINT**

Call appropriate play. Spin hand. Note section of diagram indicated by point. Your gain or loss will be in that section in the circle having the name of the play you called. E. G. To pass, spin hand, note section, look for yardage in pass circle.

Start game with kickoff from forty yard line. Person who has ball may hold card, call own plays and do their own spinning. When you get a first and ten try to call appropriate plays for advancing ball toward opponents goal. If you make ten yards or more in four or less trials you win another first and ten and retain the ball. By following football rules you will soon either score or lose ball to opponent. Record position of ball on field below

SCORING Touchdown, 6 Extra point, 1 Field goal, 3 Safety, 2.

Time of quarters, five minutes or twenty-five plays

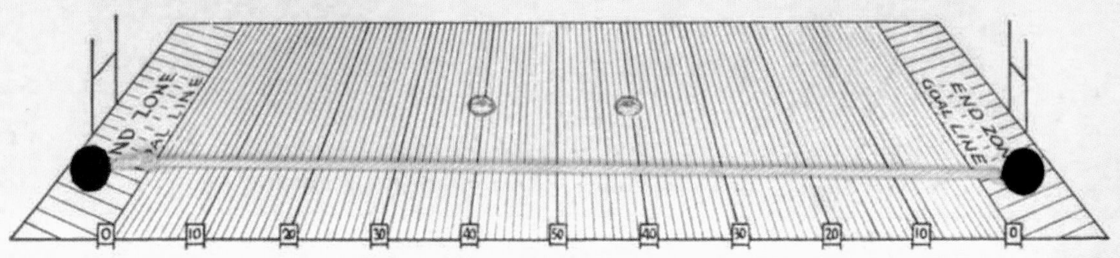

GREETINGS to the UNIVERSITY
SUCCESS to the TEAM
H.P. KAUFFMAN, City Pass. Agt.
142 So. 13th St. Lincoln
Burlington Route

ROSE PARADE
PASADENA, CALIF.
ROSE PARADE
Pasadena
1941

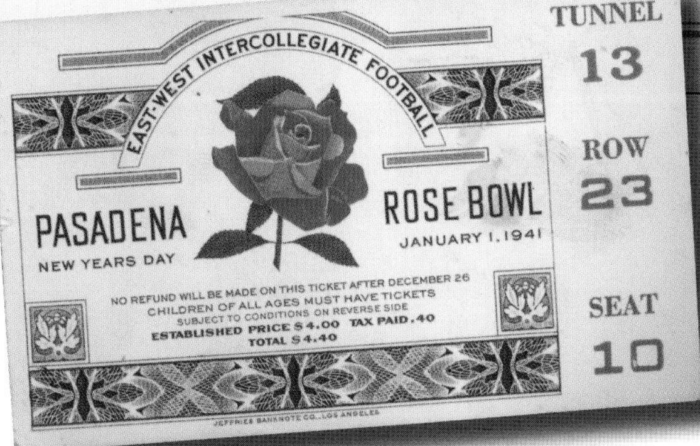
EAST-WEST INTERCOLLEGIATE FOOTBALL
PASADENA
NEW YEARS DAY
ROSE BOWL
JANUARY 1, 1941
NO REFUND WILL BE MADE ON THIS TICKET AFTER DECEMBER 26
CHILDREN OF ALL AGES MUST HAVE TICKETS
SUBJECT TO CONDITIONS ON REVERSE SIDE
ESTABLISHED PRICE $4.00 TAX PAID .40
TOTAL $4.40
TUNNEL
13
ROW
23
SEAT
10

ROSE
BOWL
BAND

CORNHUSKER SPECIALS
TO EVERY NEBRASKA HOME GAME
IOWA STATE OCT. 8
INDIANA OCT. 15
MISSOURI OCT. 29
PITTSBURGH NOV. 12
KANS. STATE NOV. 24
Burlington Route Schedules
Lv. OMAHA .... 12:05 PM
Lv. SO. OMAHA .... 12:15 PM
Ar. LINCOLN .... 1:20 PM
RETURNING SPECIAL LEAVES LINCOLN ABOUT 30 MINUTES AFTER THE GAME
A DIVERSIFIED LUNCH AND BEVERAGE SERVICE
A FAST, SMOOTH, COMFORTABLE RIDE
$1.50 ROUND TRIP
BUY YOUR TICKETS EARLY
TICKETS
City Ticket Office
16th and Farnam
or Burlington Station
PHONE AT-6831
Burlington Route
J. W. SHARPE, Gen'l Agent, Passenger Dept.

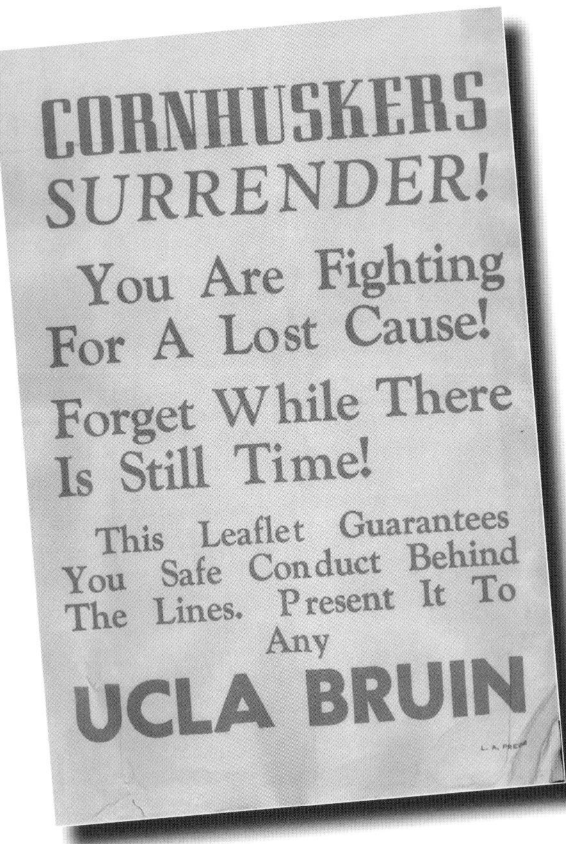

A Tribute to Football

by Grantland Rice

Blocking backs and interference—
Fifty thousand wild adherents—
Tackle thrusts and headlong clashes,
Two yard bucks and dizzy dashes,
Spiral punts and forward passes,
Run the end and hit the line,
Driving on by leg and spine,
Head and shoulder, heart and soul,
Till you fall across the goal.

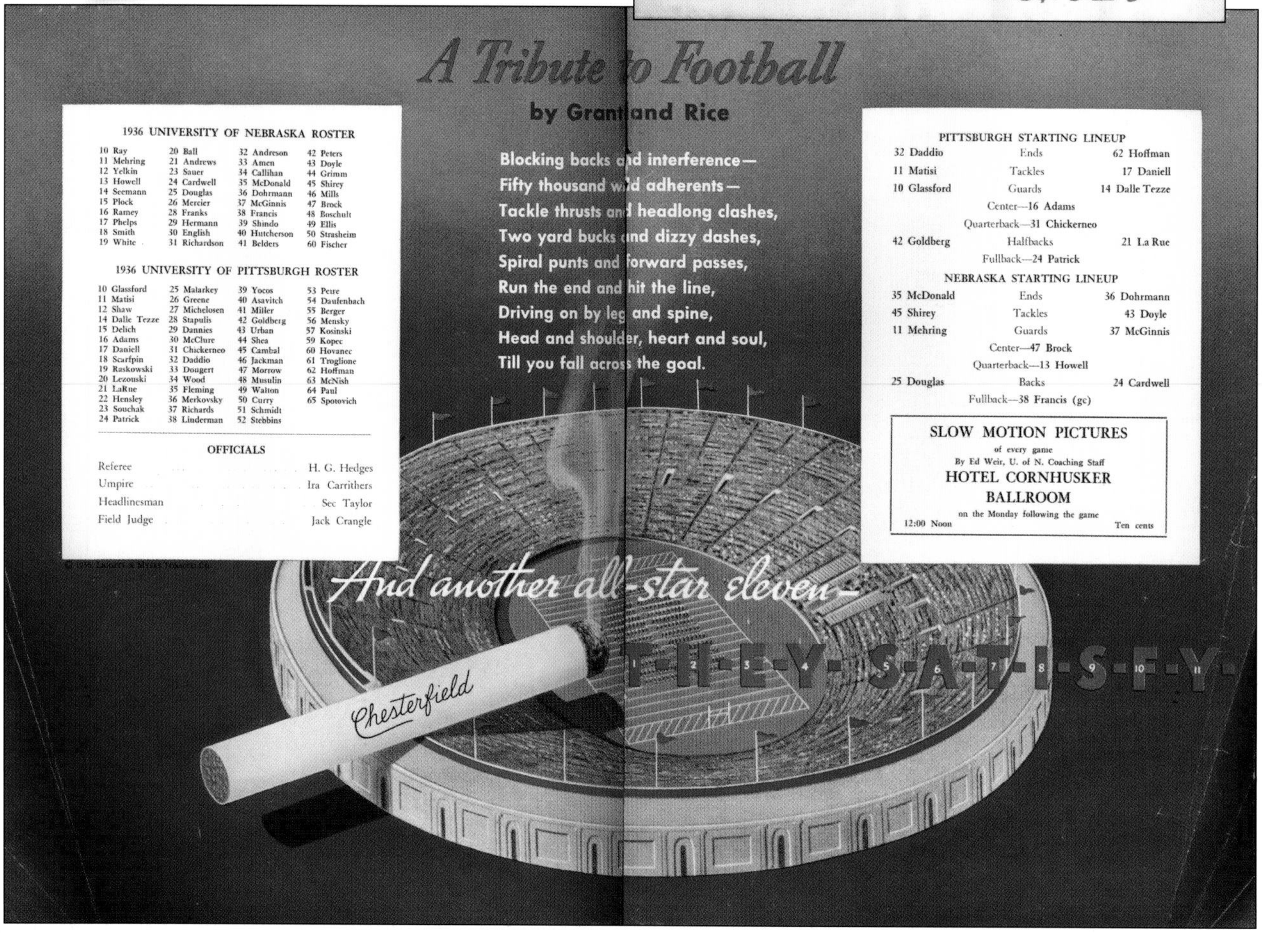

1936 UNIVERSITY OF NEBRASKA ROSTER

10 Ray	20 Ball	32 Andreson	42 Peters
11 Mehring	21 Andrews	33 Amen	43 Doyle
12 Yelkin	23 Sauer	34 Callihan	44 Grimm
13 Howell	24 Cardwell	35 McDonald	45 Shirey
14 Seemann	25 Douglas	36 Dohrmann	46 Mills
15 Plock	26 Mercier	37 McGinnis	47 Brock
16 Ramey	28 Franks	38 Francis	48 Boschult
17 Phelps	29 Hermann	39 Shindo	49 Ellis
18 Smith	30 English	40 Hutcherson	50 Strasheim
19 White	31 Richardson	41 Belders	60 Fischer

1936 UNIVERSITY OF PITTSBURGH ROSTER

10 Glassford	25 Malarkey	39 Yocos	53 Petre
11 Matisi	26 Greene	40 Asavitch	54 Daufenbach
12 Shaw	27 Michelosen	41 Miller	55 Berger
14 Dalle Tezze	28 Stapulis	42 Goldberg	56 Mensky
15 Delich	29 Dannies	43 Urban	57 Kosinski
16 Adams	30 McClure	44 Shea	59 Kopec
17 Daniell	31 Chickerneo	45 Cambal	60 Hovanec
18 Scarfpin	32 Daddio	46 Jackman	61 Troglione
19 Raskowski	33 Dougert	47 Morrow	62 Hoffman
20 Lezouski	34 Wood	48 Musulin	63 McNish
21 LaRue	35 Fleming	49 Walton	64 Paul
22 Hensley	36 Merkovsky	50 Curry	65 Spotovich
23 Souchak	37 Richards	51 Schmidt	
24 Patrick	38 Linderman	52 Stebbins	

OFFICIALS

Referee	H. G. Hedges
Umpire	Ira Carrithers
Headlinesman	Sec Taylor
Field Judge	Jack Crangle

PITTSBURGH STARTING LINEUP

32 Daddio	Ends	62 Hoffman
11 Matisi	Tackles	17 Daniell
10 Glassford	Guards	14 Dalle Tezze
	Center—16 Adams	
	Quarterback—31 Chickerneo	
42 Goldberg	Halfbacks	21 La Rue
	Fullback—24 Patrick	

NEBRASKA STARTING LINEUP

35 McDonald	Ends	36 Dohrmann
45 Shirey	Tackles	43 Doyle
11 Mehring	Guards	37 McGinnis
	Center—47 Brock	
	Quarterback—13 Howell	
25 Douglas	Backs	24 Cardwell
	Fullback—38 Francis (gc)	

SLOW MOTION PICTURES
of every game
By Ed Weir, U. of N. Coaching Staff
HOTEL CORNHUSKER BALLROOM
on the Monday following the game
12:00 Noon — Ten cents

And another all-star eleven—

T-H-E-Y S-A-T-I-S-F-Y

Chesterfield

U. N.
IN COMMEMORATION OF THE MEN OF NEBRASKA WHO SERVED AND FELL IN THE NATIONS WARS
CHRISTIANSEN
TERRY TOWNSEND
TALES OF THE CORNHUSKERS
MORIAL STADIUM 1936
TSBURGH ★ NEBRASKA
1942
N
IN COMMEMORATION OF THE MEN OF NEBRASKA WHO SERVED AND FELL IN THE NATIONS WARS
Tales of the Cornhuskers
Missouri-Nebraska
U.S. NAVY
MISSOURI
vs.
NEBRASKA
Saturday, October 27, 1945
MEMORIAL STADIUM
COLUMBIA, MISSOURI
PRICE 25c
NAVY DAY

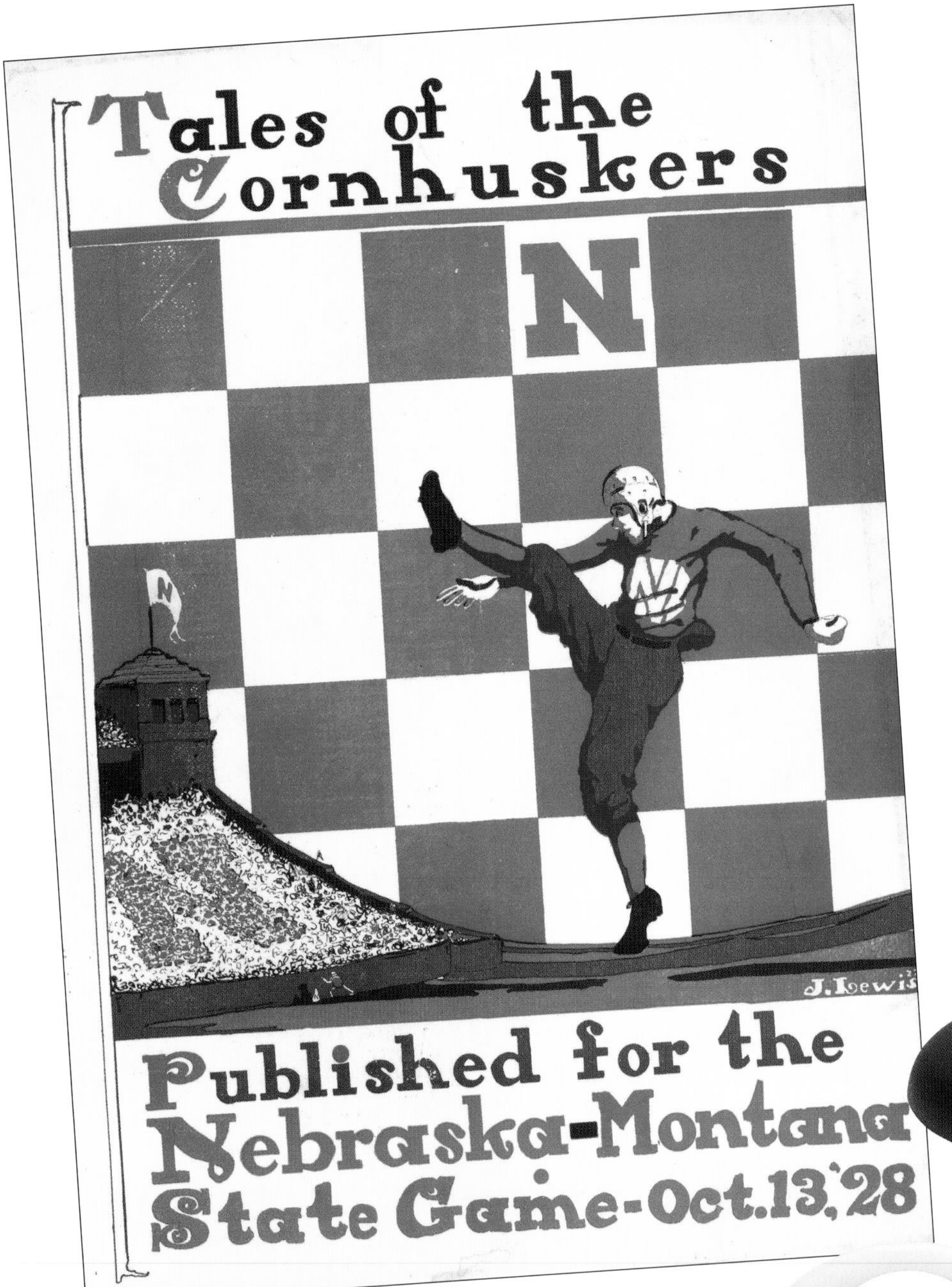

Tales of the Cornhuskers

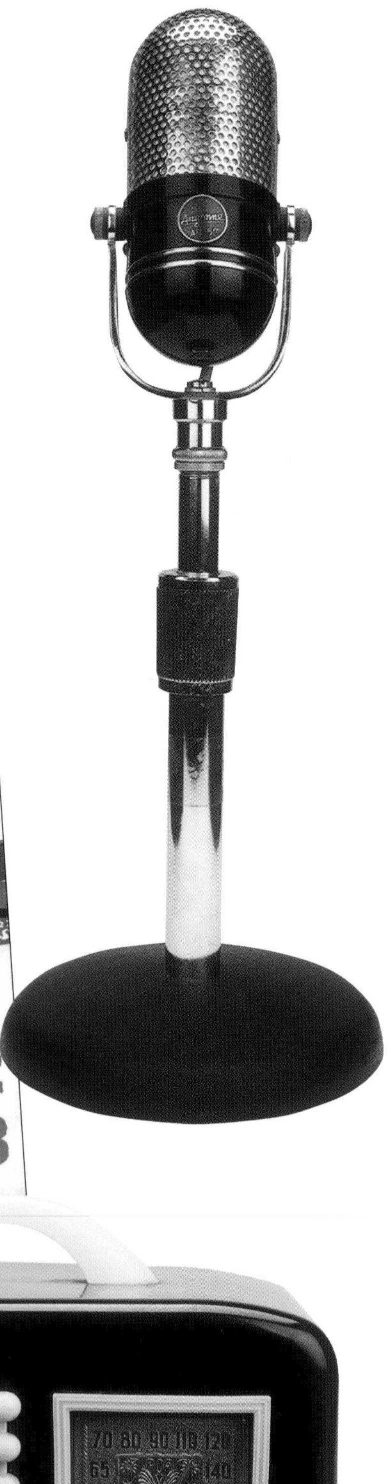

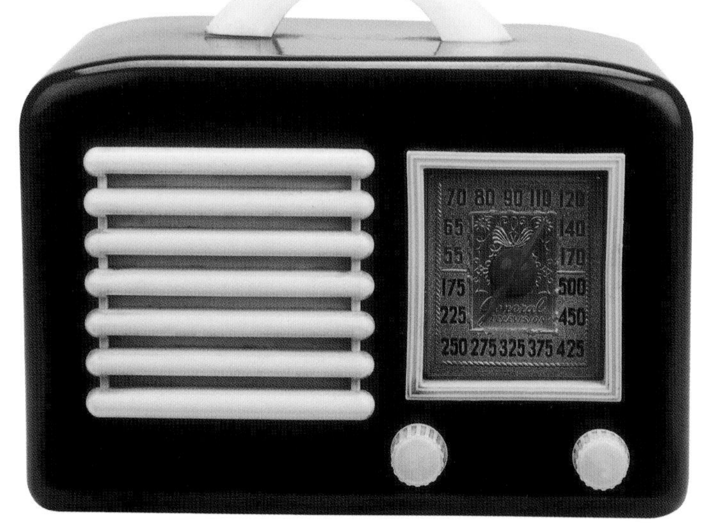

The Nebraska Alumnus
Homecoming Issue
October 1932
WAL IF PRICES GO UP!
KIN I GO?
CORN
THE PRESS PRESSING
OWW!
I JUST GOTTA SEE IT!
FRENZIED WILDCAT ROOTER
DANA X
FIE ON MR SELLECK
HOMECOMING DANCE TONIGHT COLISEUM
'RAY
'RAH
MEMORIAL STADIUM
BAGS OF GOLD
JOHN K. SELLECK
"INDIAN SCHULTE"
DOUGH
HI GUY!
RAY RAMSAY
CHEMISTRY
U HALL
OLD GRADS
NEBRASKA HALL
NEW PAVING
WELCOME GRADS
"PREXY" NED ABBOTT
FORMER MUSEUM
"STEAM ROLLER" HAROLD HOLTZ
BESSEY
STOP PIMPLE
MAWL
OH YEAH?
GRANT MEMORIAL
GIT OUTTA THAR!
A BIG BUMFIRE
MORE PIMPLES
TO HOMECOMING FROLIC
MORRILL
DEAN THOMPSON "INSTRUCTING" A FRESHMAN
PHARMACY
BILLY QUICK
EH?
I SAY!
COME - PAPA'LL SHOW YOU WHERE HE MET MAMA
FANCY MEETING YOU - HERE
WELCOME GRADS!
CLASS OF '98 MEETS THE CLASS OF '99
OUCH
ANDREWS
SOCIAL SCIENCES
ZZZZ
YOUNG GRADS HAVING A GO AT COLLEGE AGAIN
HEY! STOP BLOCKING TRAFFIC
HI WILD CATS
I WANTA BALOON
WE'LL ALL STICK TO-GETH-A-
HE RETURNED TO RELIVE THE "GUD" OLD DAZE!
UNROMANTIC SOUL
OLD GRAD PAINTING CAMPUS RED
TEACHERS
POLICE
H'M'M'M
OLD GRADS
DEAN HEPPNER
OLD PATRIARK
ROOF CUT AWAY TO SHOW EDITOR NORLING HARD AT WORK
TEMPLE
HURRY UP DEAR!
WELCOME WILDCATS
By JAMES H. PICKERING AN OLD GRAD HIMSELF

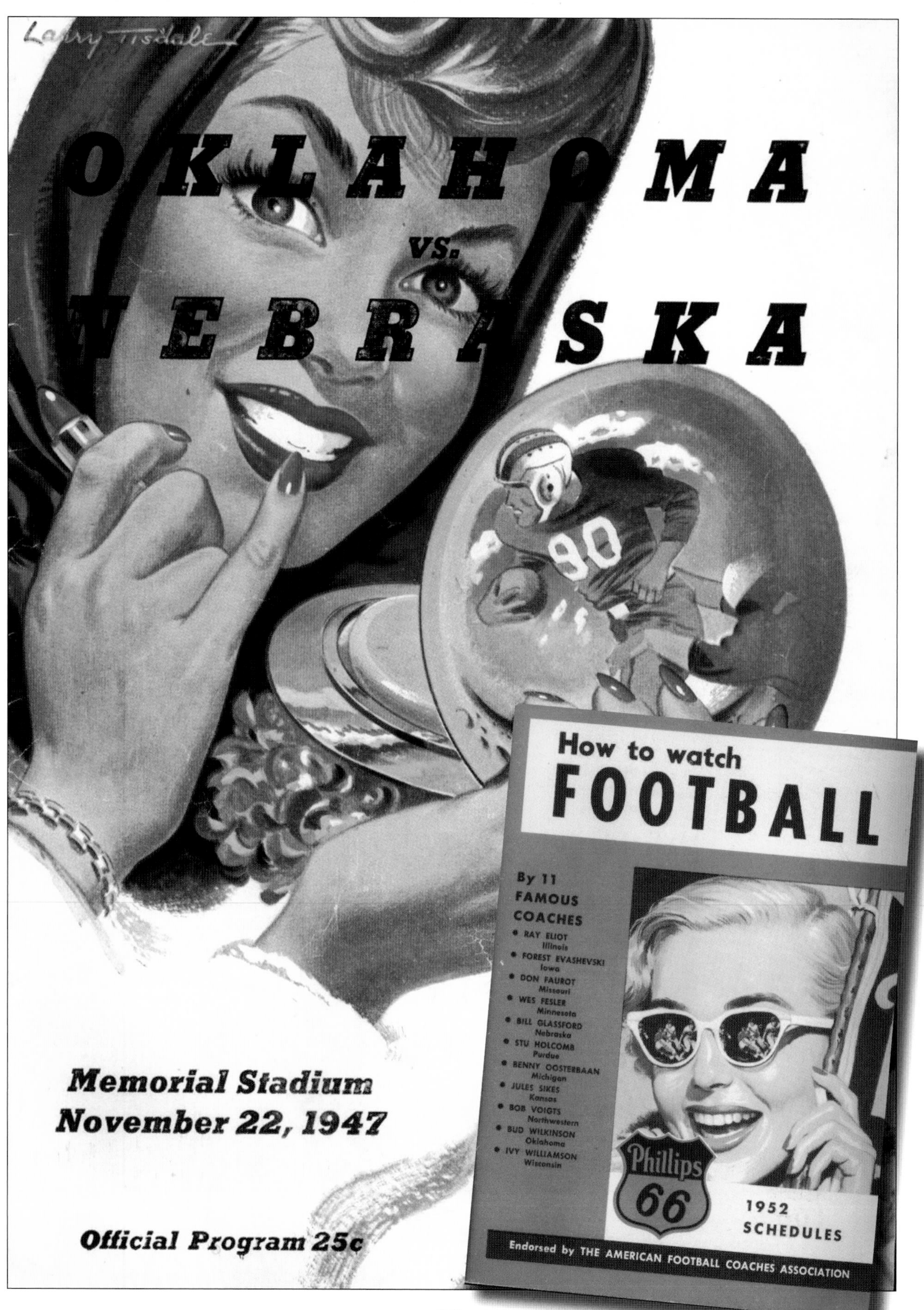
OKLAHOMA
vs.
NEBRASKA
Memorial Stadium
November 22, 1947
Official Program 25c
How to watch
FOOTBALL
By 11
FAMOUS
COACHES
• RAY ELIOT
Illinois
• FOREST EVASHEVSKI
Iowa
• DON FAUROT
Missouri
• WES FESLER
Minnesota
• BILL GLASSFORD
Nebraska
• STU HOLCOMB
Purdue
• BENNY OOSTERBAAN
Michigan
• JULES SIKES
Kansas
• BOB VOIGTS
Northwestern
• BUD WILKINSON
Oklahoma
• IVY WILLIAMSON
Wisconsin
Phillips
66
1952
SCHEDULES
Endorsed by THE AMERICAN FOOTBALL COACHES ASSOCIATION

TWENTY-FIRST ANNUAL
Orange Bowl
CLASSIC
IOWA ST.
MARYLAND
VIRGINIA
WAKE FOREST
OLORADO
NEBRASKA
N.C. STATE
K. STATE
MISSOURI
DUKE
KANSAS
N. CAROLINA
OKLAHOMA
CLEMSON
S. CAROLINA
DUKE
VS.
NEBRASKA
ORANGE BOWL STADIUM
MIAMI, FLORIDA
BOB LAMME

NEBRASKA vs OKLAHOMA

Official Program 25 *cents*

Probable U. C. L. A. Lineup

LH	FB	RH
Johnson 17	Steffen 19	Rowland 25

LE	QB	RE
Clements 49	Nagel 37	Tinsley 15

LT	LG	C	RG	RT
Matthews 50	Dimitro 27	McLaughlin 10	Nikcevich 66	Pastre 69

SQUAD LIST

3 Stamper, b	26 Thompson, t	45 Riggs, e
5 Brown, Jim, t	27 Dimitro, g	46 Way, t
6 Braly, b	29 Hunt, e	47 O'Meara, b
9 Schroeder, b	30 Wilkinson, e	49 Clements, e
10 McLaughlin, c	31 Simpson, g	50 Matthews, t
12 Lewis, t	33 Lampkin, b	51 Brown, Jack, b
15 Tinsley, e	34 Hansen, b	52 Stroschein, t
16 Raffee, g	35 Vujovich, c	56 Steiner, g
17 Johnson, b	36 Eaton, g	58 Giovinazzo, b
18 Duffy, b	37 Nagel, b	62 Murphy, b
19 Steffen, b	39 Short, b	64 MacLachlan, g
21 Jenson, t	40 Hale, c	65 Lewand, g
22 Debrow, e	42 Cogswell, e	66 Nikcevich, g
24 Halopoff, b	43 Polizzi, b	68 Brown, G., e
25 Rowland, b	44 Howe, e	69 Pastre, t

OFFICIALS

Referee—Louis House, William Jewell
Umpire—Alan Williams, Cornell

SCORE	1	2	3	4	TOTAL
U.C.L.A.					
NEBRASKA					

Probable NEBRASKA Lineup

LH	FB	RH
K. Fischer 15	Collopy 28	Mueller 23

LE	QB	RE
Fletcher 34	Costello 12	B. Schneider 36

LT	LG	C	RG	RT
Toogood 64	Salestrom 18	Novak 61	Means 10	Sedlacek 24

SQUAD LIST

10 Means, g	28 Collopy, b	49 Goeglein, t
11 Bostwick, e	29 DiBiase, g	50 Meyer, b
12 Costello, c	32 Moore, b	51 Hazen, e
13 Bauer, b	33 Ferguson, b	52 Myers, b
14 C. Fischer, b	34 Fletcher, e	53 Pizinger, g
15 K. Fischer, b	36 R. Schneider, e	54 Sailors, e
16 Spellman, c	38 Godfrey, t	55 D. Schneider, b
17 Mullen, c	39 Harkrader, g	56 Strasheim, b
18 Salestrom, g	40 Golan, t	57 Reese, t
20 Ackerman, b	41 Wiegand, b	60 Story, b
21 Damkroger, e	42 Moomey, b	61 Novak, b
23 Mueller, b	43 Hawkins, b	62 Cochrane, e
24 Sedlacek, t	44 Lee, b	63 Hutton, b
25 Bloom, b	45 Magsamen, e	64 Toogood, t
26 Dorn, t	46 Young, b	
27 Lipps, g	48 McGill, c	

OFFICIALS

Field Judge—Dick Sklar, Kansas
Head Linesman—William Simas, St. Mary's

GET EDDIE DOOLEY'S FOOTBALL PRE
Chesterfield Supper Club Every Fri

KANSAS STATE vs. NEBRASKA
MEMORIAL STADIUM
OCTOBER 5, 1946
Larry Tisdale
OFFICIAL 25¢ PROGRAM
THE
SUGAR BOWL
NEBRASKA
NEW ORLEANS, LA
NEBRASKA
BIG
RED
GO
N

POPCORN 15¢
N
1957-'58
1
Member
"EXTRA POINT
CLUB"
Miller & Paine
NEBRASKA
Landmark
FOOTBALL DAY MENU
STRICT ENFORCEMENT OF THE STATE LIQUOR LAW IN REFERENCE TO
MIXING OF DRINKS IS ADHERED TO BY THE MANAGEMENT.
WE APPRECIATE YOUR COOPERATION.
Kindly confine your choice to this menu to expedite service
(PLEASE DO NOT ASK FOR SUBSTITUTIONS)
DINNER
Served from 5 to 10 P. M.
PRICE OF ENTREE INCLUDES ROLLS, BUTTER AND BEVERAGE
Fresh Shrimp Cocktail 60
Fruit Cocktail 30
Fresh Garden Vegetable Soup 15-25
Relish Tray
ROAST STUFFED YOUNG TOM TURKEY, Giblet Gravy and Cranberry Sauce 1.95
FRESH INDIVIDUAL COLORADO MOUNTAIN TROUT, Lemon Butter 1.95
BROILED CORNHUSKER SPECIAL CLUB STEAK, Colbert 2.95
ROAST PRIME RIB OF CORN FED BEEF au Jus 2.50
GRILLED SELECT CALF LIVER STEAK, Canadian Bacon 1.95
Butter Browned Potatoes
Green Beans in Butter
Salad Bowl
Coffee
Butter
Rolls
Fresh Apple Pie 15
Grapenut Pudding 15
French Pastry 20
Brownie a la Mode 30
Cherry Frosted White Cake 15
Fresh Strawberry Sundae 30
Chocolate Sundae 25
Liederkranz Cheese, Crackers 35
Pumpkin Pie 15
Sherbet 15
Ice Cream 15
SATURDAY, NOVEMBER 14, 1953
COLORADO
VS.
NEBRASKA
2 P. M. MEMORIAL STADIUM
HOTEL
CORNHUSKER
UNDER SCHIMMEL DIRECTION
LINCOLN, NEBRASKA

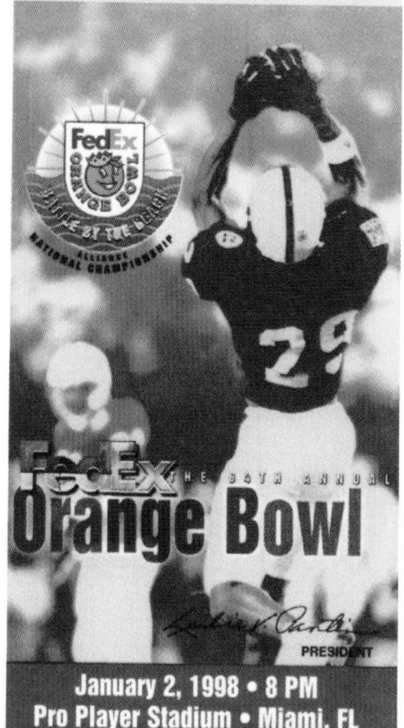

2009 RE-ENTRY PASS

OKLAHOMA
NOVEMBER 7, 2009

TICKET STUB MUST BE PRESENTED WITH THIS
RE-ENTRY PASS FOR READMITTANCE

HUSKERS.COM

SOUTH STADIUM-GATE A or B
16B2 96 32
SEC. ROW SEAT
NEBRASKA
1974 FOOTBALL
FACULTY - EMPLOYEE TICKET
DEPARTMENT OF ATHLETICS
$25.50
INCLUDING SALES TAX
TICKETS WILL NOT BE REPLACED
NOT TRANSFERABLE
NO REFUND
This ticket is subject to confiscation by the NEBRASKA ATHLETIC DEPT. if used by any person other than the original purchaser.
Must be signed in ink SIGNATURE
3 4 5 6 7 8 9 10
38th ANNUAL COTTON BO Classic
TUESDAY JANUARY 1 1974
DALLAS COTTON BOWL
PAGEANTRY 12:15 P. M.
RESERVED
ADMISSION $8.00
COTTON BOWL CLASSIC JAN. 1, 1974-1:10 P.M.
ENTER GATE F
SEC. ROW SEAT
229 2 16
ACCT# 20854 PRICE: $45.00
THE COLLEGIATE COLLISION
WESTERN STAR TRUCKS CLASSIC
CHAIRMAN, PRESIDENT & CEO
FREE! 30 BLUE STAM
Any Blue Stamp merchant will re this ticket for 30 Community Blue S
FILLED BOOKS ARE WO
$2.50 in Merchand
$2.00 in Cash
Stamps of blue buy more f
NEBRASKA'S NUMBER ONE S
COMMUNITY SAVINGS STAMP
NEBRASKA MEMORIAL STADIUM
SATURDAY • OCTOBER 3, 1998 • 1:00 PM
ARROWHEAD STADIUM
GAME TIME SUBJECT TO CHANGE
NEBRASKA MEMORIAL STADIUM
EAST STADIUM
WEST STADIUM
MINNESOTA
WEST STADIUM 10th STREET ENTRANCE
SEC. ROW SEAT
31 21 26
Versus MINNESOTA
SAT., SEPT. 24,
RESERVED
STAIRWAY 10
ROW 56
SEAT 103
USC VS NEBRASKA
FOOTBALL 1970
L.A. COLISEUM / SAT., SEPT. 19 / 8 P.M.
ESTABLISHED PRICE $6.00
FedEx ORANGE BOWL
MIAMI, FLORIDA
NORTH SIDE $42.00
Kickoff CLASSIC THE MEADOWLANDS
MON. AUG. 29, 1983—9 PM
NEBRASKA
OKLAHO vs NEBRASKA
Incl. Sales Tax
SAT., NOV. 11, 1978—1:30 P.M.
NO REFUND — HOLD YOUR OWN TICKET
GO BIG RED!
NEBRASKA 17 OKLAHOMA 14
MEMORIAL STADIUM
25th YEAR TOM OSBORNE
THE NATION'S WINNINGEST COACH
OKLAHOMA
SAT., NOV. 1, 1997
Memorial Stadium
Lincoln, Nebraska
GATE SEC. ROW SEAT
9 129 11 17
WEST STAD. RAMP 25-27
25 11 17
SAT NOV 19
COLORADO
NEBRASKA
FOOTBALL
UNIVERSITY OF NEBRASKA versus COLORADO
Est. Price $2.50 Federal Tax .50 $3.00
NO REFUND
MEMORIAL STADIUM
1949

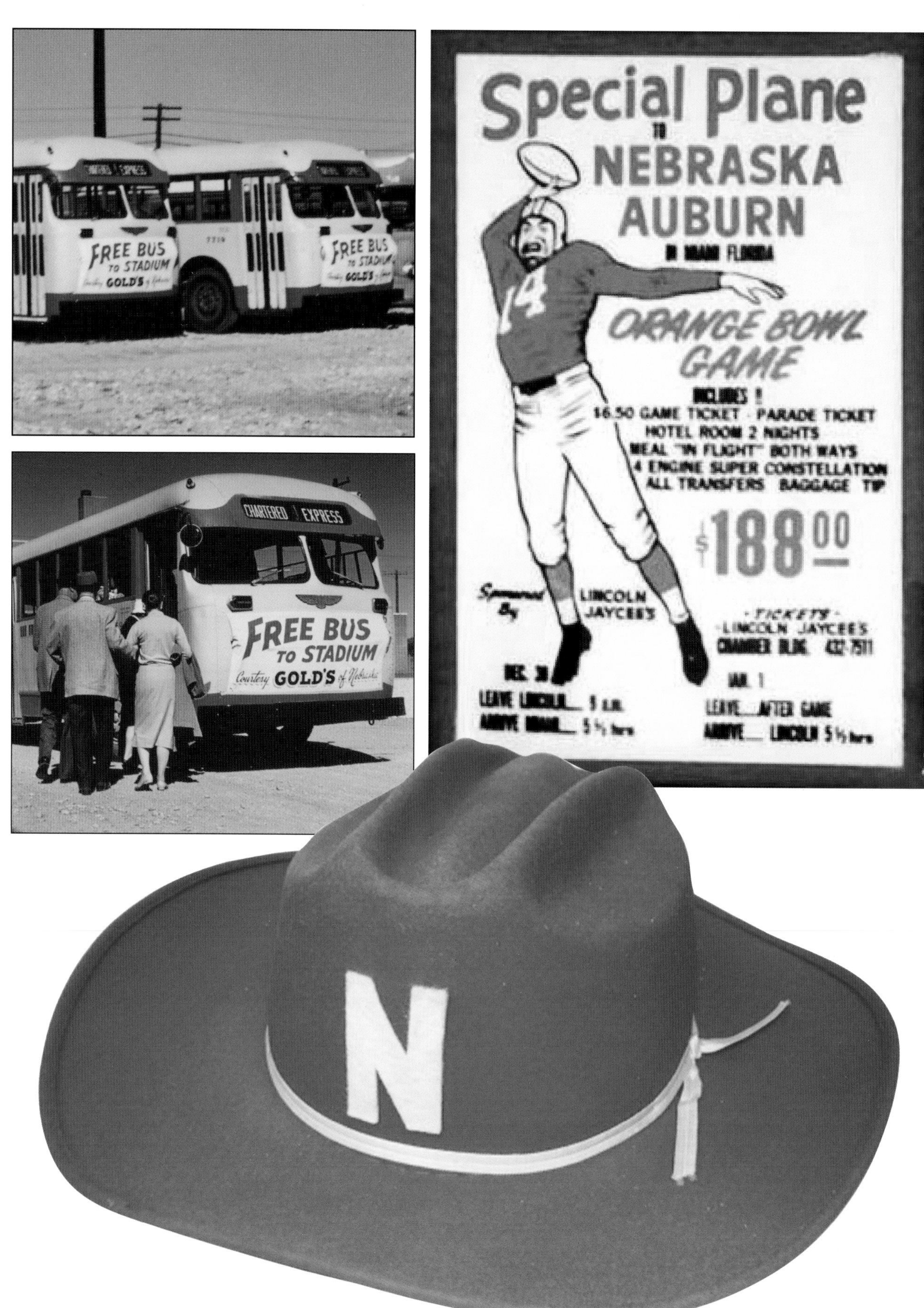
FREE BUS
TO STADIUM
Courtesy GOLD'S of Nebraska
CHARTERED EXPRESS
Special Plane
TO
NEBRASKA
AUBURN
ORANGE BOWL
GAME
16.50 GAME TICKET · PARADE TICKET
HOTEL ROOM 2 NIGHTS
MEAL "IN FLIGHT" BOTH WAYS
4 ENGINE SUPER CONSTELLATION
ALL TRANSFERS BAGGAGE TIP
$188.00
LINCOLN
JAYCEE'S
LINCOLN JAYCEE'S

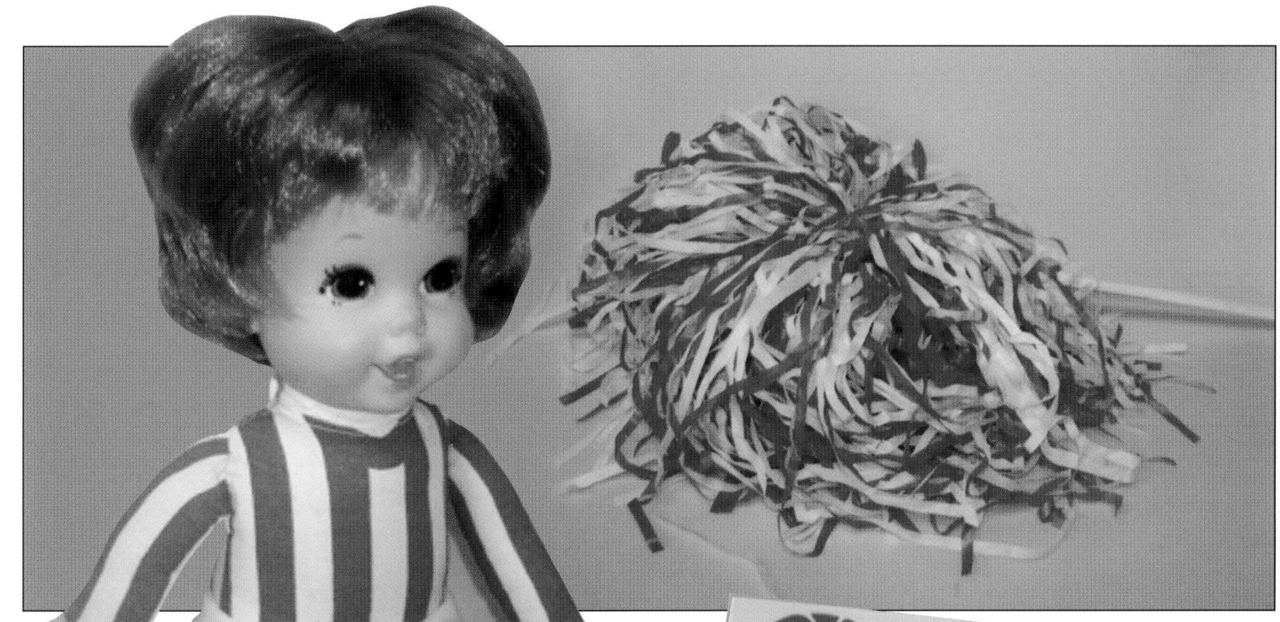

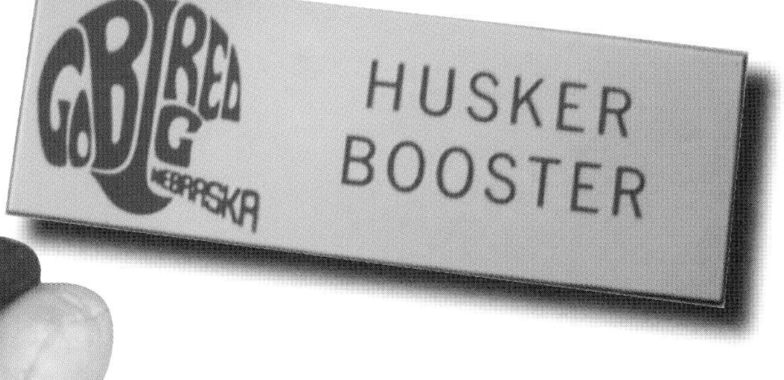
GO BIG RED NEBRASKA
HUSKER BOOSTER

NEBRASKA
CORNHUSKERS

VALENTINO'S
"the Greatest Italian Food West of Naples"

A CLAYTON MOTEL
Clayton HOUSE

N
GO!
BIG RED

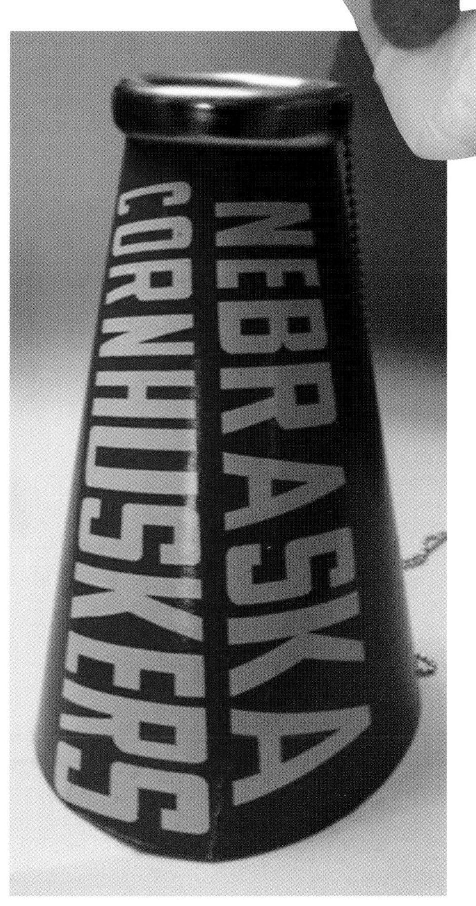

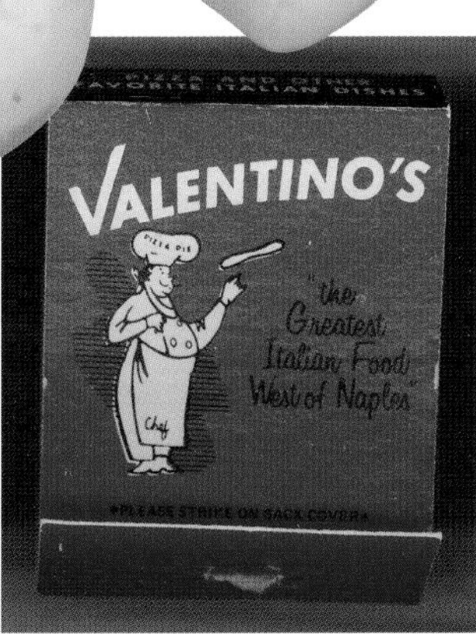

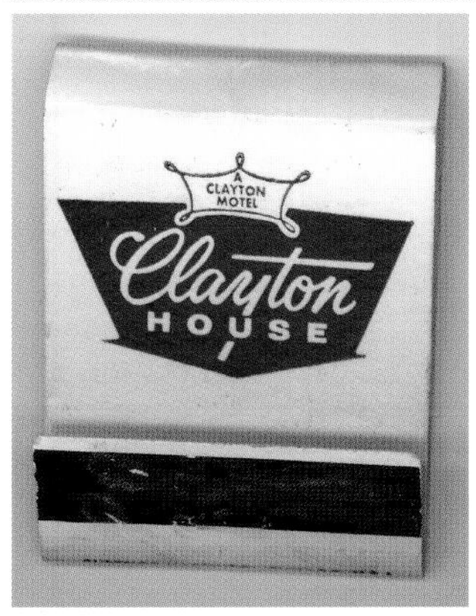

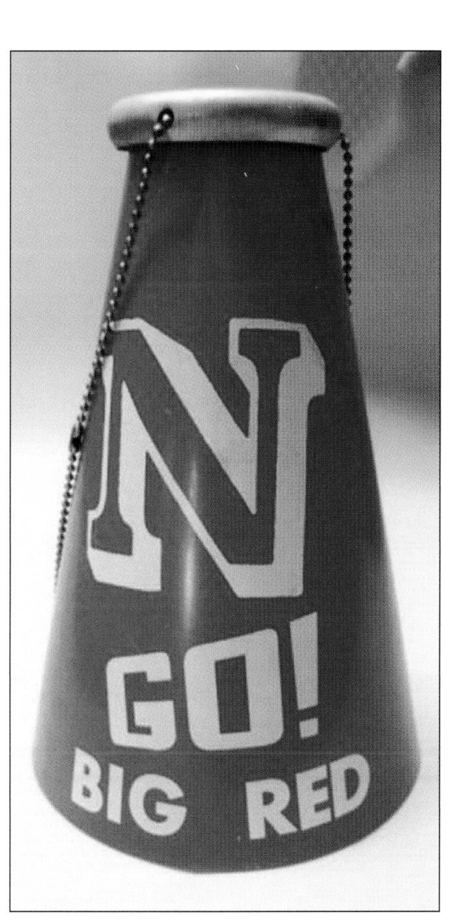

NEBRASKA

GO BIG RED

"GO BIG RED!"
BIG 8 CONFERENCE
COLLEGE FOOTBALL
NEBRASKA CORNHUSKERS
SCHEDULE
1971
NEBRASKA FOOTBALL
1971 SCHEDULE
SEPT. 11—OREGON
SEPT. 18—MINNESOTA
SEPT. 25—TEXAS A&M
OCT. 2—UTAH STATE
OCT. 9—At MISSOURI
OCT. 16—KANSAS
OCT. 23—At OKLAHOMA STATE
OCT. 30—COLORADO
NOV. 6—IOWA STATE
NOV. 13—At KANSAS STATE
NOV. 25—At OKLAHOMA
DEC. 4—At HAWAII

N

GO
BIG RED
NEBRASKA
GO
BIG RED
NEBRASKA

HUSKER
12
A Champion
in Flavor

TIME OUT!
BEFORE YOU BUY, SEE YOUR CHRYSLER-PLYMOUTH OR DODGE DEALER
...BE THE CENTER OF ATTENTION IN A NEW CAR FROM CHRYSLER CORPORATION!
WHAT A LINE! PLYMOUTH, DODGE, CHRYSLER, IMPERIAL, SIMCA OR SUNBEAM
THEY GRAB YOU!
TRIPLE THREAT!
CHRYSLER CORPORATION, LONG ON STYLING, LONG ON FEATURES AND ON ENGINEERING
Plymouth • Dodge • Chrysler • Imperial • Dodge Trucks • Simca • Sunbeam
CHRYSLER CORPORATION
SEE THE AFL IN ACTION EACH WEEK ON NBC-TV.

COLORADO BUFFALOES
IOWA STATE CYCLONES
KU
KANSAS JAYHAWKS
KSU
KANSAS STATE WILDCATS
MISSOURI TIGERS
N
NEBRASKA CORNHUSKERS
SOONERS
OKLAHOMA SOONERS
OSU
OKLAHOMA STATE COWBOYS
★--Night Games
1974 SCHEDULE
Pull tab, 1974 schedule will appear in window when black dot is opposite team. 1973 record appears in window on reverse side.
© 1974, Joe Kelly
P.O. Box 13
Gadsden, AL. 35902
PULL TAB
BIG-8 CONFERENCE SLIDE-GUIDE TM

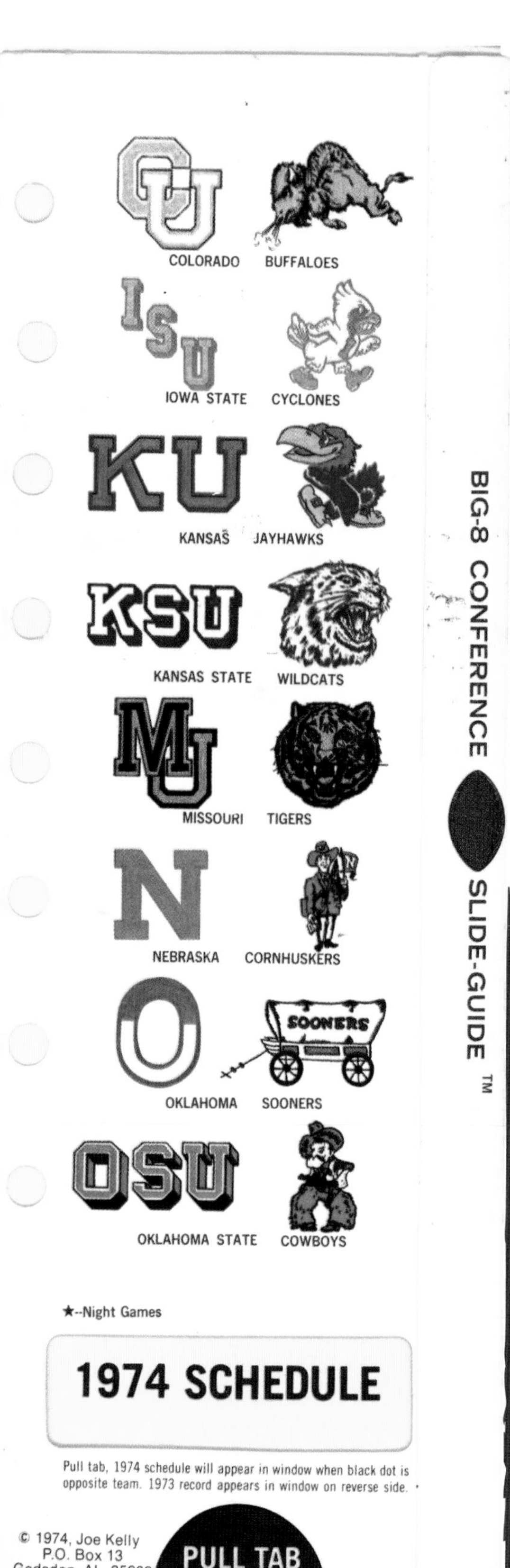

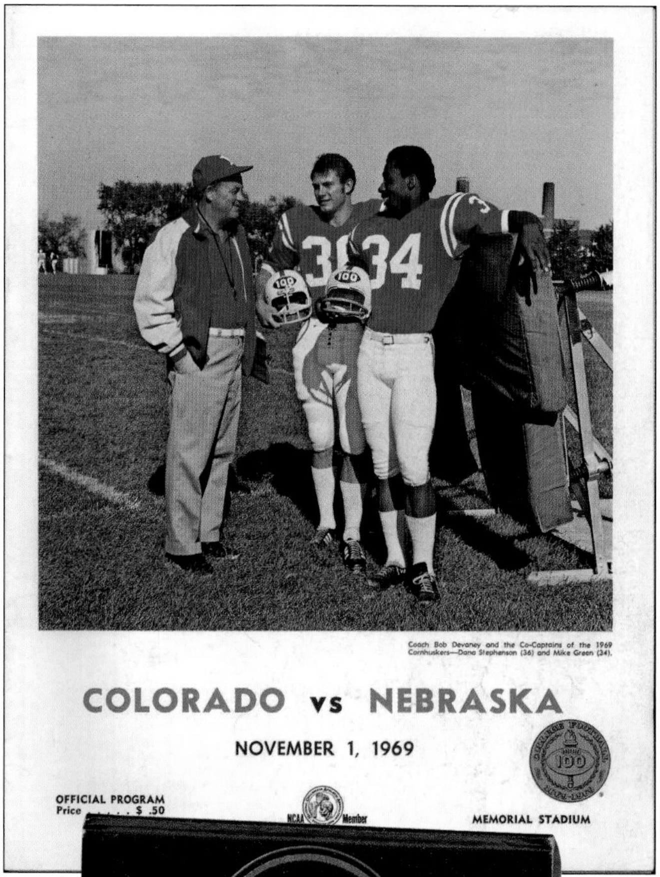

Coach Bob Devaney and the Co-Captains of the 1969 Cornhuskers—Dana Stephenson (36) and Mike Green (34).
COLORADO vs NEBRASKA
NOVEMBER 1, 1969
OFFICIAL PROGRAM
Price . . . . . $ .50
NCAA Member
MEMORIAL STADIUM

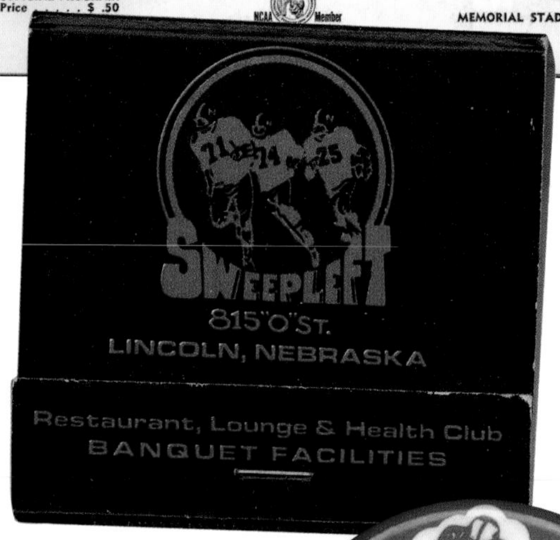

SWEEPLEFT
815 "O" ST.
LINCOLN, NEBRASKA
Restaurant, Lounge & Health Club
BANQUET FACILITIES

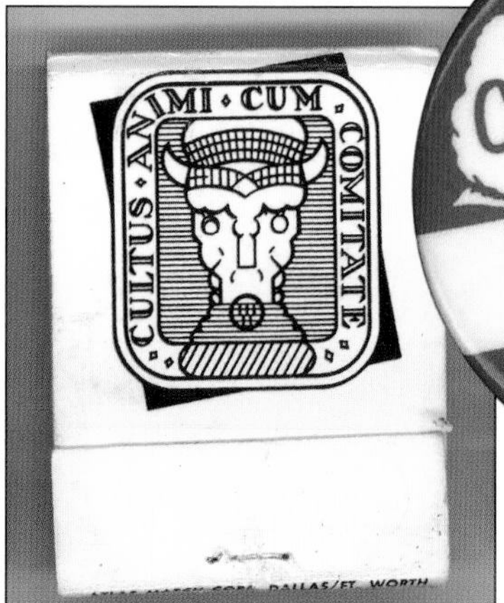

CULTUS · ANIMI · CUM · COMITATE

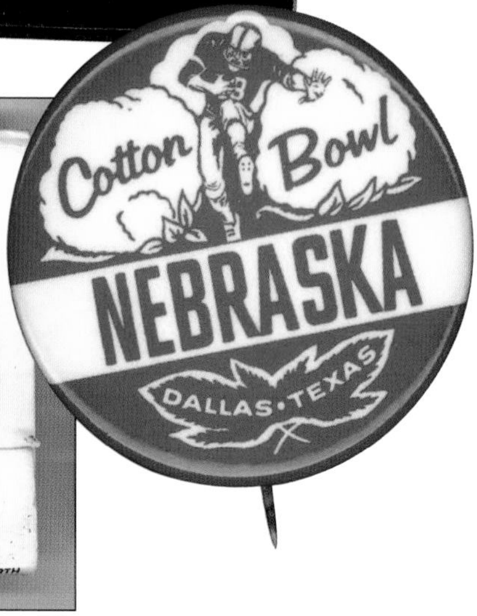

Cotton Bowl
NEBRASKA
DALLAS · TEXAS

N
N
14
35
81
75
98
NTL CHAMPION
NEBRASKA UNION
on the Cornhusker Campus
N
GO TEAM
N
N

OKLAHOMA STATE vs NEBRASKA

OCTOBER 25, 1969

OFFICIAL PROGRAM
Price . . . . . $ .50
(Tax Included)

MEMORIAL STADIUM

©Pepsi

NEBRASKA 1
NATIONAL CHAMPS

NEBRASKA
NATIONAL COLLEGIATE CHAMPIONS
1970-1971
N
GO BIG RED
CORNHUSKERS

100
THE UNIVERSITY OF NEBRASKA
CENTENNIAL
1869-1969

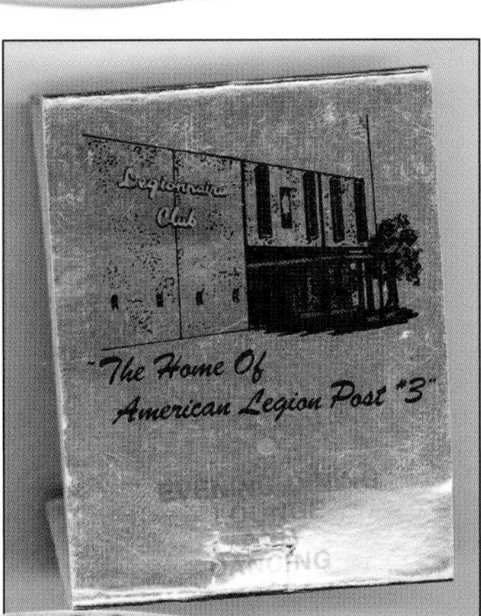
"The Home Of
American Legion Post "3"

University of Nebraska
Official Alumni
ORANGE BOWL TOUR
JANUARY 1, 1982
Name
Address
GO BIG RED

Holler
"ya-hooo!
Mountain
Dew"
There's a bang
in ever' bottle!

Lasting Traditions

Red and white balloons flying high over Memorial Stadium following the initial score of any game, and a hot dog with mustard.

Memorial Stadium housed 54,000 fans in 1965.

UNIVERSITY OF NEBRASKA
19
N
63
USHER

Things go better with Coke.
Coca-Cola
Coke
GO BIG RED
N
UNDEFEATED 1965
ORANGE BOWL
N
GO BIG RED
ORANGE BOWL - 1966
N
GO BIG RED

N
WATCH
"the BOB DEVANEY SHOW"
12-NOON
SUNDAYS
SEE — COACH BOB DEVANEY and Exclusive, FULL-COLOR, GAME-ACTION films . . . every Sunday noon . . . of all 10 Husker games.
HEAR — Coach Devaney's comments on the game highlights and opponents for the following weeks' games.
Host . . . Veteran Sportscaster Joe Patrick
You're "IN," with these "behind the game" facts about BIG-RED FOOTBALL, over these stations . . . on Nebraska's "FIRST Football TV NETWORK"
KETV-7* OMAHA
KOLN TV-10 LINCOLN
KGIN TV-11 GRAND ISLAND
KHOL TV-13 KEARNEY
KHPL TV-6 HAYS CENTER
KHTL TV-4 SUPERIOR
KHQL TV-8 ALBION
* Originating station.
UNIVERSITAS NEBRASKENSIS
FEB. 15, 1869.
DIAMOND MATCH DIV ◆ OMAHA NEBRASKA
OFFICIAL KFOR CORNHUSKER FAN
NU
N

20
JOHNNY RODGERS
TROPHY WINNER
No.1
NEBR. #1-1970. GO BIG RED
1
Go BIG RED
NEBRASKA
KENTUCKY STRAIGHT
BOURBON
100
NATIONAL CHAMPIONS
NEBRASKA
1970
1971

MISTY
iversity of Nebrask
FALSTAFF
National Champions 1970
Lincoln Hotel
Victorian Charm
JAMES D. RODNEY - Gen. Mgr.
In State 180 at 9th
LINCOLN, NEBRASKA

Memorable Mascots

We're not really sure how many folks remember Johnny Husker, but as recently as the 60s, he was still wearing a pair of coveralls on the sidelines. In the 1970s, a cartoonist in Texas dreamed up "Herbie" for the Cotton Bowl match-up...and, so far as we know, He's still handing out hugs...AND slugs!

There is no official symbol of a Cornhusker and various cartoonists have caricatured the mystical something that typifies Nebraska football - some winning fan approval and others arousing fan ire.

The cartoon character, "Herbie Husker," evolved out of Nebraska's trip to the 1974 Cotton Bowl in Dallas. Artist Dirk West of Lubbock, Texas, designed a Cornhusker cartoon for the Cotton Bowl press headquarters that caught the eye of former Husker SID Don Bryant. Later, Bryant contacted West for permission to use the cartoon, and West expressed a desire to refine his original cartoon and improve some of the character's features. As a result, West was commissioned to draw an original Cornhusker cartoon character that served as a mascot for all Husker athletic teams.

"Herbie" is the registered logo of the Cornhusker Athletic Department, which controls its use. West's concept of Nebraska football is appropriate -a burly, rugged and confident fellow who is proud of both the athletic and the agricultural traditions of the University of Nebraska. The new Herbie made his debut prior to the Huskers' 2003 season opener against Oklahoma State.

In 2006, Herbie was named the national mascot of the year, continuing an outstanding tradition of excellence by the Nebraska Spirit Squads and Mascots.

In recent years, the University has used the Cornhuskers' football helmet superimposed on a script "Huskers" for a football logo, and eight years ago, NU unveiled a block N logo with a script "Huskers." Both are registered trademarks of the Athletic Department. Although Nebraska has continued to make improvements and changes into the coming century, it also takes great pride in its history, so quite fittingly, "Bugeaters" has also been registered for exclusive use by the University of Nebraska.

Huskers NSide
Courtesy of
University of Nebraska

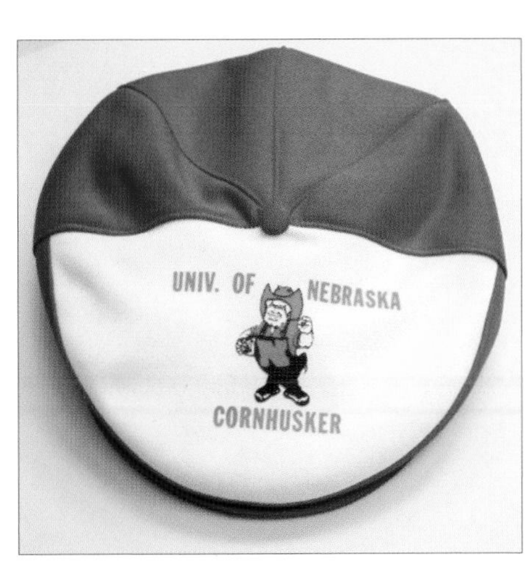

Hold 'em Blackshirts!
We Want A Touchdown!
Beat the Buffs!
Go Huskers Go!
We're Number 1!
Beat Ok-la-ho-ma!
GO BIG RED!

CHAPTER SIX

The Nifty Fifties

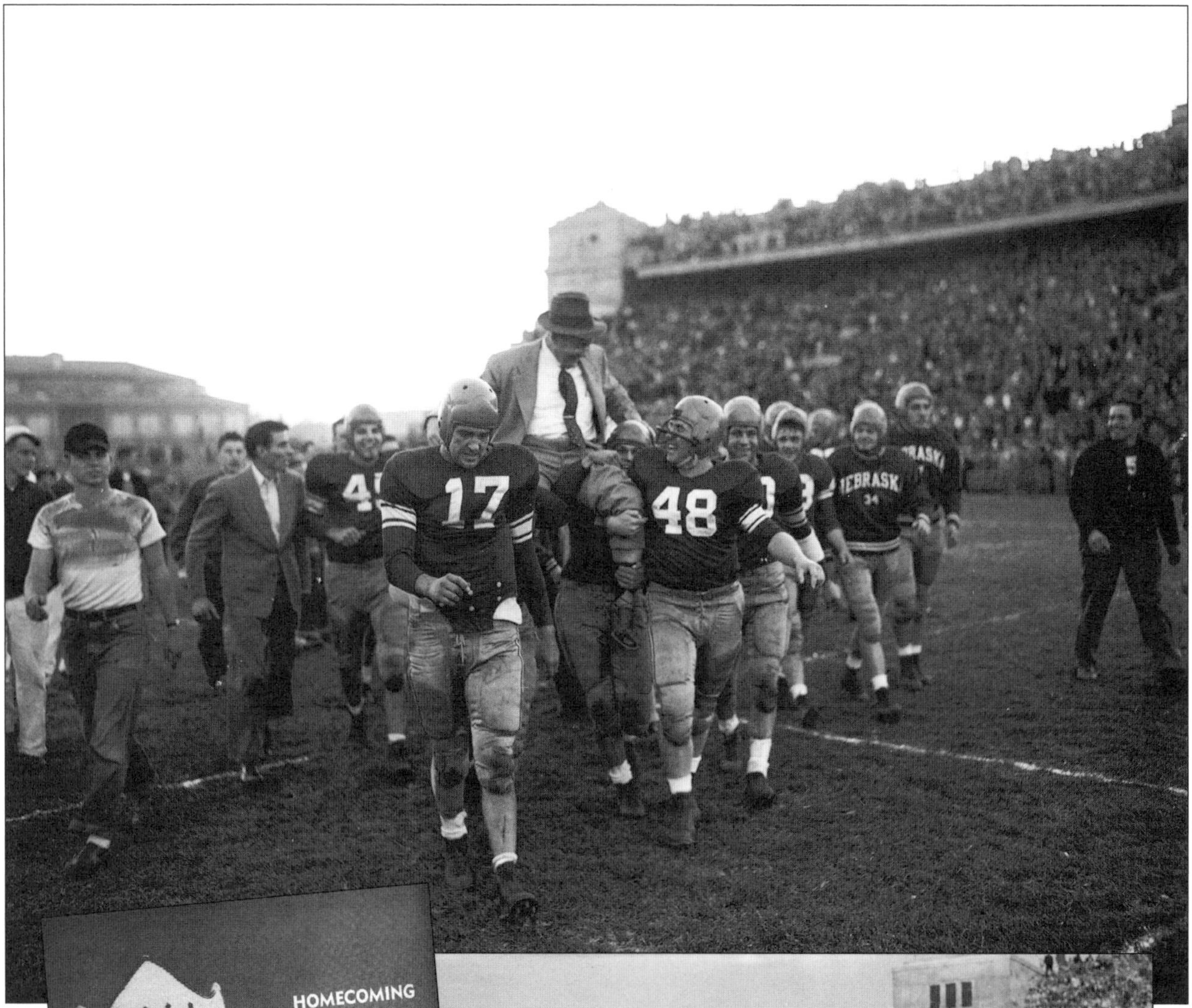

HOMECOMING
QUEEN
Shirley Allen

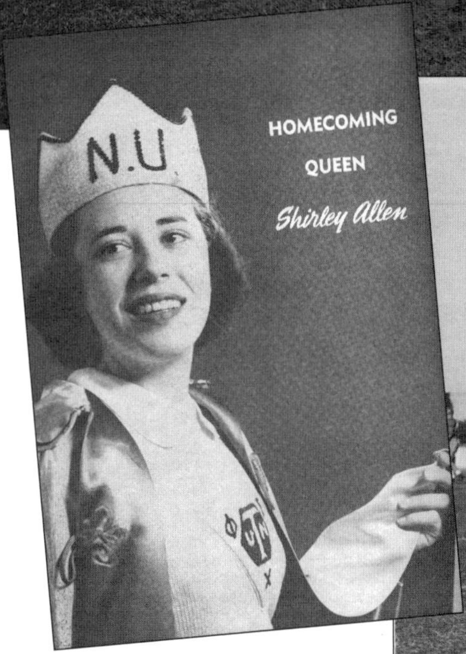

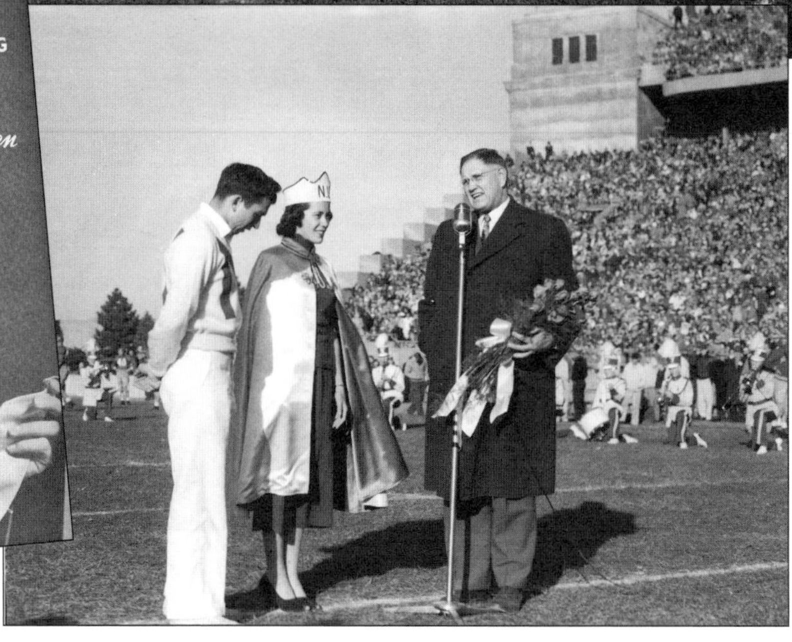

Keeping Score

In the early '50s, as a high schooler, I had a job at Magee's, working in the window dressing department. Part of my job on game day Saturday was to keep track of the scores of important football games around the country, including Nebraska, and then run up and post them on a big chart in the front window. This way, the downtown shopping crowds could keep track of their favorite teams.

As a child in the 40s, I remember being downtown on game Saturdays, and the men's and woman's pep clubs (the Kernels and Tassels) handed out long feathers with a big "N"sticker on them (to wear on your lapel). I think those were free. They also sold balloons and red or white carnations adorned with a chenille (pipe cleaner) "N" on the surface. But the most marvelous of all were the huge white mums with big red chenille "N's" on them! Back then, all the games started at the same time in the early afternoon, so crowds of people were downtown on O Street shopping and eating before the game.

Now people park their cars somewhere downtown and flow in a solid stream of red straight north to the stadium on 10th and 11th Streets.

Joyce Donlan

Game Day Diary

October 24, 1957

Saturday morning Mr. Editor and his wife turned three sleepy boys over to the loving care of Grandma Benson; kissed them once, twice, thrice; and set out for a carefree trip to Lincoln and the football game.

The sky was a blazing pink and the sun hadn't yet shown his face. It was a sight we two don't often see. Simply because – the day is well begun before our household rolls out of bed.

The miles passed by rapidly...big black birds swooped down to the highways for their scavengers' breakfasts...the green fields looked out of place in October...fall flower were blooming in every town – lavender chrysanthemums, scarlet zinnias...there was a monkey statuette gazing out a picture window in Grand Island.

Pheasants were cockily strutting through the fields – probably seeking good hiding spots for the hunting season.

Farmers were looking at their corn and a few were picking it.

There were fishermen on the bridge who must have gotten up even earlier than we.

By York, we saw a bright, blue plane near a hangar...near Lincoln, a shiny jet buzzed over our heads.

We were standing downtown watching the many bands marching on their last few blocks of the parade. They looked exhausted but happy after the long trek.

At last – we were at the football game overseeing a mass of many hues as the bands sat at either end of the stadium.

The scarlet and cream players dashed onto the field…the drums rolled…the team moved down the field.

The ball was kicked…everyone cheered…and Nebraska lost to Syracuse 9 to 26!

-Gwen

October 31, 1957

We've heard people comment that we were too young to be publishing a paper, but with a newspaper to print, and our three growing boys to raise, we figure in ten years we'll be twenty years older.

-Gwen

October 19, 1961

The Better Half was making his choice between two new hats for the wife. "Get that one. The other makes you look like an old woman!"

That one was a frothy, frilly, bright aqua creation from Reier's made of dyed chicken feathers. It was comfortable, big, striking, wiggly, and you could hide straight hair or even pin curls under it…if you didn't mind looking through fluff to see where you were going!

But where to wear it?

Church was out. Who wants to sit up front at the piano and compete with the minister for attention?

The chance came last Saturday when we journeyed to Lincoln for the football game.

"No one will notice in that crowd of people", mistakenly thought I.

Well, let me tell you, they did notice. And it was kind of fun. The hat got those first looks…then the second stares (of amazement?)…that are given to beautiful women and odd-looking hats. (Don't ask me which.)

Men looked, then looked again, then sort of laughed, or asked "What is it?" Women looked, then said " Like your chapeau, it could knock anybody out"…"It's different anyway"…. or "I just wish I had the nerve to wear one like it."

(They didn't realize that I won't have the nerve to wear it again.)

But the school boys were the most truthful in their comments. Riding up the escalator I cold hear a group behind me deciding which one was going to "bomb" it with a spitball.

And a little boy at the stadium took one look and murmured "Gee…Cotton Candy!"

The sight of green hair, pink hair, a hat just covered with bright blue flowers, and one that Dick described as a "missile launcher" bolstered my courage.

But the clincher was to see the Governor's wife, Mrs. Frank Morrison, pass by our section attired in a big, striking, bright aqua, frilly creation.

Only hers was fashioned of fur…not dyed chicken feathers.

- Gwen

November 30, 1961

Didn't wear that hat to the Colorado-Nebraska football game a couple weeks ago. It's not that I don't like it…just couldn't get up the nerve to be looked at again.

(The mousey anonymity suited me better.)

Dick's loyalty to his alma mater, Colorado usually wells up in him as the band plays "Glory, Glory Colorado." Being in the presence of two fellow Coloradoans (his brother Don and wife Althea) bolsters his CU patriotism.

This year it was different.

After conning him into buying me a Nebraska corsage, I was amazed to hear him cheer at the Huskers' one good play early in the game.

"Guess that cinches it. I'm a full-fledged Nebraskan now. Maybe it was because Colorado didn't bring along their band or something."

He might have been tempted to change his loyalty by the time the contest came to a dismal end.

Big Red's failure to cross the fifty-yard line caused one dim viewer to comment: "No hits, no runs, no errors."

November 2, 1967

CAR 54, WHERE ARE YOU?

It was 11:22 in the first quarter of the Nebraska-Minnesota game and the Nebraska announcer asked, "Will the owner of car, license number, blank, blank, blank, please report to your car…(pause)…it is on fire."

Another pause and he continued, " Not only is it on fire but it is locked!"

Friend-Husband decided if he were the owner, he'd just stay seated.

October 31, 1963

Secretary of Commerce Luther Hodges took a back seat to another celebrity at the Nebraska-Colorado football game last weekend.

Everyone applauded when Hodges' name was announced over the speaker…but the star of the show was Nebraska's own Robert Taylor.

You know how it is when the loudspeaker booms, "Will movie-tv actor Robert Taylor please stand up!" Correct…every other person in the stadium rises to get a better look and no on gets a good view.

Mr. Taylor, star of "The Detectives," was seated just 15 rows from us in the adjacent section…and, Girls, let me tell you…!

He's just as handsome as in the movies or on television. His hair might be a little grayer…but still not as metallic as Friend-Husband's looks.

For the rest of the game the binoculars, which the hubbies had been using to watch the huskers, were confiscated by their wives for a better glimpse at their favorite movie star.

Gwen Lindberg

Girls? Knot Interested.

In 1955, when I was 11 years of age: Before the stadium was enclosed there were bleachers at the north and south ends of the football field called the knot hole sections. It cost 50 cents for students to get in. Boys had to sit at the south end and girls had to sit on the north end. The boys' section was always full - there weren't many on the girls' end.

Clark Splichal

Those WEREN'T The Days

Probably my greatest game day memory concerns the preparation for the game rather than the game itself. The game was homecoming 1958 and was won by Missouri 35 to 0. The customary for that time was "3 yards and a cloud of dust" offense by the Huskers and not much better defense! Ah those WEREN'T the days!!

In preparation for the game, I was able to purchase four tickets for that game - three days before the game - at the ticket office. The seats were in the east stadium - on the 40 yard line (south) about half way up.

If I remember the cost for those four seats was under $25.00. That's what made the day memorable for me! Not much of a football game for Nebraska fans, but the seats didn't cost an arm and a leg at least!!

Aren't we all glad for the major changes that followed a few years later with the coming of Bob Devaney and his memorable team of coaches. Maybe this is an example of the old saying "Mighty oaks from tiny acorns grow"!

Thanks for the opportunity to share this one. There have been many games to follow that were more enjoyable to watch but your first game should always stick in your mind. By the way, the coach was "hung in effigy" in the homecoming celebrations that followed the game somewhere on campus.

John Linhardt

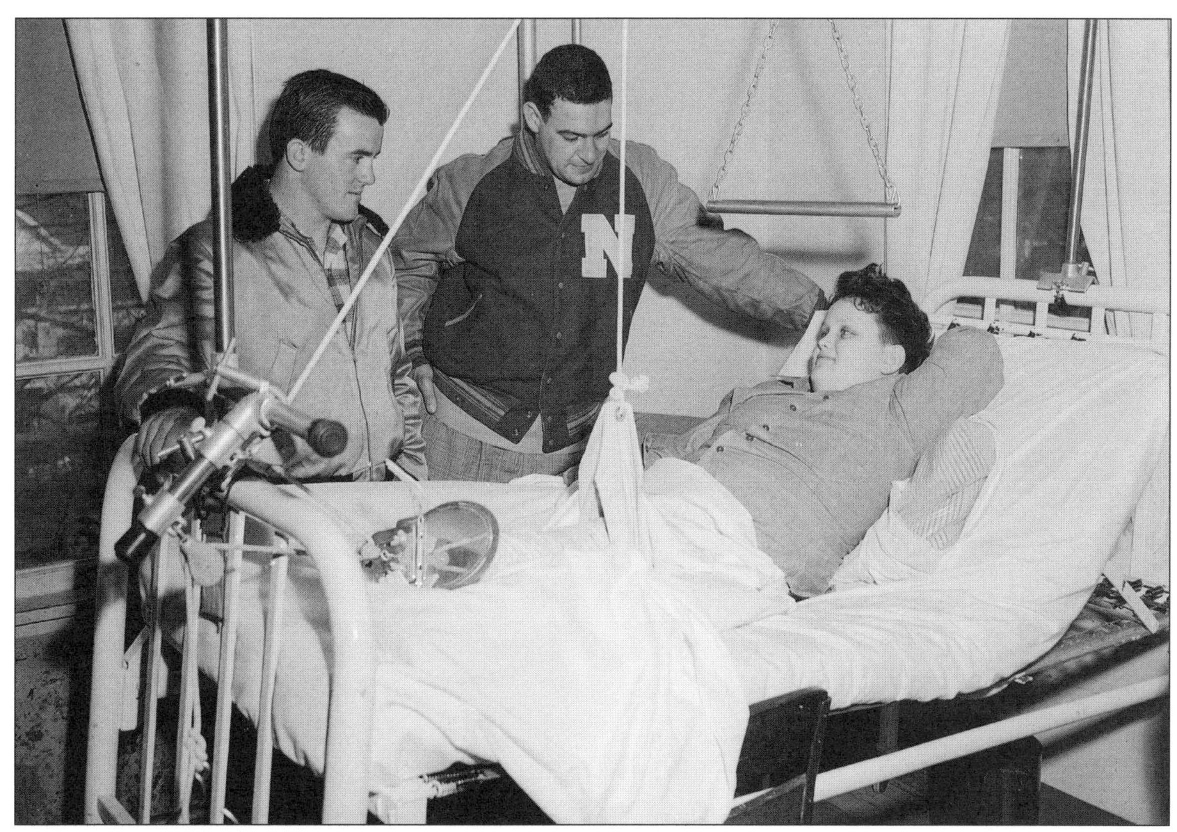

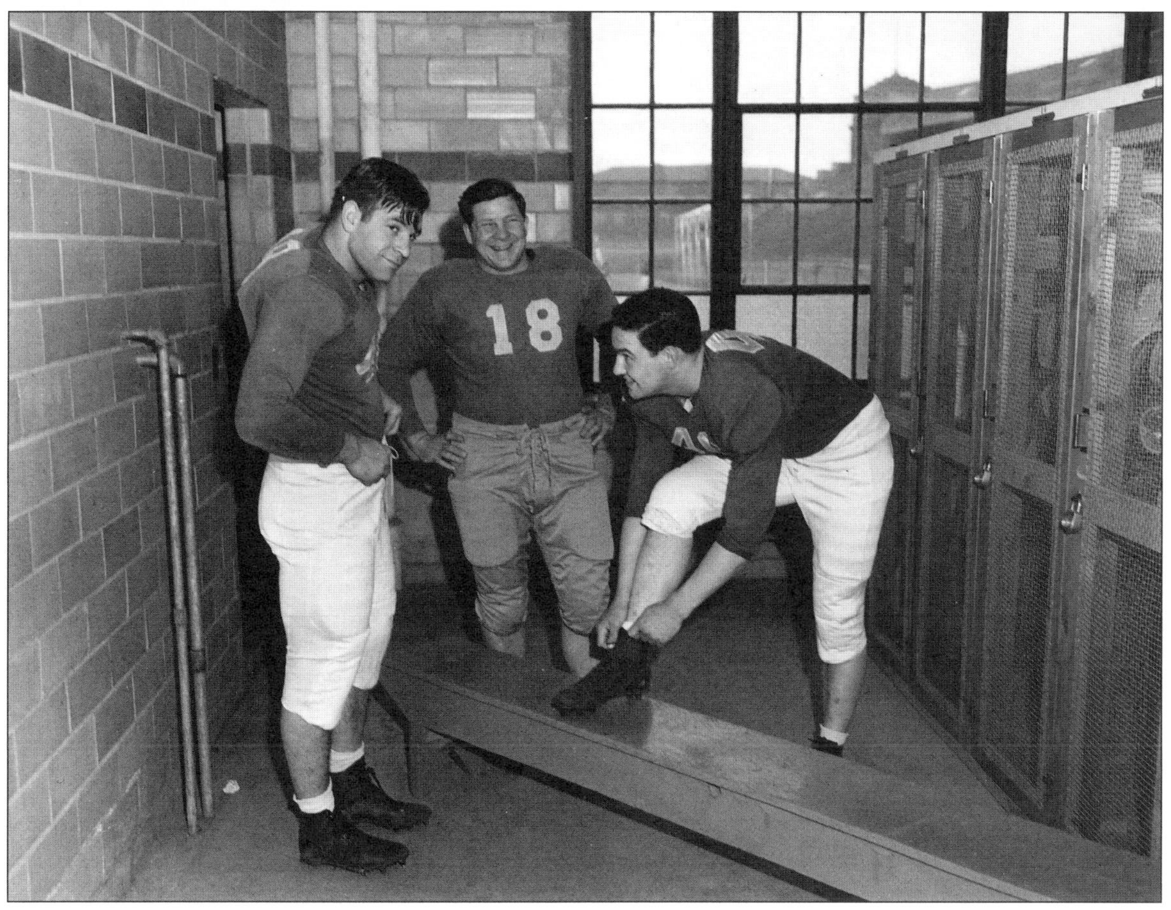
18

MEMORIAL STADIUM OF THE UNIVERSITY OF NEBRASKA MCMXXIII

We're OUT TO BEAT THE FIGURES OF 1951
GOLD'S LENDING LIBRARY ONLY 1¢ DAY
Street

Football Memories

I have fond memories of growing up in Lincoln on football Saturdays. I loved the big mums and carnations with the pipe cleaner N's on them, the ladies wearing their flowers downtown, and the excitement in the air.

I went to a small parochial school close to downtown. They distributed Knot Hole tickets for 50 cents each for the football games. On Saturday morning my best friend and her Dad (who were also my cousin and uncle) would pick me up and we would go to my Grandmothers. My grandparents had 14 children, so I had lots and lots of first cousins growing up and there was always lots of people around. Grandmas yard always looked like a parking lot.

The family owned the farm on Sun Valley Boulevard that sat right under the underpass north of "O" Street. We would pile out of the car and go in to see Grandma. She always baked Runzas on Saturdays and she would give us kids a runza for each pocket to keep our hands warm when we walked to the game. We would cross the road and walk across the railroad bridge spanning Salt Creek and across the open land to the stadium for the game. The Knot Hole section was the bleachers that made up the north stadium in those days. Brrrr!

I love the memory of those cold days walking to and attending the football games. I don't remember how many games Nebraska won or lost, but I remember in the '50s the excitement of football Saturdays and hands warm from Runzas handed out at Grandmas. Happy times.

Midge Alfieri

Concession Price List

1958

PROGRAMS	25c	COLD DRINKS	15c
BACK RESTS	35c	HOT DOGS	25c
CIGARETTES	30c	PEANUTS	15c
SANDWICHES	25c	ICE CREAM BARS	10c
CRACKERJACK	10c	COFFEE	10c
APPLES	10c	CANDY BARS	10c
EYE SHADES	15c	POTATO CHIPS	10c
POPCORN (Megaphone)	15c	COTTON CANDY	10c
POPCORN (Bag)	10c	GUM	10c
TAFFY APPLES	15c	CIGARS	15c

ASPIRIN 15c

All concessions in the Stadium are operated by the Athletic Department.
All profits go for aid to Cornhusker athletes.
Your patronage is appreciated.

L. F. KLEIN
Director of Concessions

News Flash: Sooner "Magic" Momentarily Disrupted!

This is a slice of the goalpost from the "biggest" Nebraska football game ever! This game ended the longest conference unbeaten streak in NCAA history...74 consecutive games. It was the first time we'd beaten Oklahoma in 17 years and the first time ANY team in the conference had beaten OU in 13 years, so it was a happy day for the whole Big Eight Conference. The win over OU was by far the biggest. The University called off school the following Monday.

The goalposts came down at the end of the game and were paraded down "O" street. As a money-maker, the University sliced up the goalposts and sold them.

It just happened to be Halloween day (my birthday), and when we went out that night, at every house we went to... instead of saying "trick or treat", we said "YEA NEBRASKA!"

It was a great day for Nebraska football.

Tom Hinds

Chapter Seven

The Times They Are A-Changin'

NU Band Day – A Memorable Experience

On October 17, 1953, I woke up with the roosters. My Fairbury High School band was invited to perform at the University of Nebraska Band Day that day. I quickly dressed, grabbed my clarinet, and drove to Fairbury. Even though I arrived early, many seats in the chartered buses were taken.

I rushed onto one of the buses and plopped into a front seat ... and felt something squish beneath me. I bounced back up and realized that I had just sat on a hat belonging to our band director's wife. How embarrassing! I apologized to Mrs. Foust and then searched for a truly empty seat.

The hat incident didn't keep me from being excited about the day ahead. In the 1950s, performing during a University of Nebraska football game was a dream for all the state high school band members. Since 1938, (except for cancellations in 1943 and 1944, during World War II) the half-time show has featured musicians performing the length and breadth of the entire football field.

Our band arrived in Lincoln, registered by 8 a.m. and then headed to the staging area on 10th street to line up for the traditional 9:30 a.m. downtown parade. Our Fairbury band uniforms stood out with our short military-style jackets trimmed in gold. Our hats featured white plumes. Our trousers were crimson with a white stripe. Our drum major and twirlers wore white trousers with a crimson stripe. The rhythm of the drums complemented the rhythm of nearly 200 "taps" of the metal plates attached to the heels of our white shoes. We marched south from the UNL downtown campus to O Street, marching from 10th to 14th Street on O Street, then back to the stadium. The parade was strictly limited to one hour.

At the stadium, we joined the other 60-some bands, composed of more than 3000 members, to practice for our half-time performance on the main field. (We were lucky. Applications from about 50 other bands were turned down because of lack of space.) Participation was limited to 3,600 students – the number of seats in the north and south end zone bleachers. These same seats composed the knothole section except for one game a year for Band Day.

At noon, we enjoyed a lunch served south of the main field, provided by the Lincoln Chamber of Commerce. After a fun lunch, we located our seats for the 2:00 p.m. game and impatiently waited for our half-time performance. Truthfully, it didn't matter to me whom the Nebraska football team played that day. Actually, I don't remember much at all about the game. But I do remember the awesome experience of playing "The Star Spangled Banner" with the other 64 bands, led by the University Band. My band, along with all the others, created a huge mass band playing as one. Under the direction of Donald A. Lentz, conductor of the U.N. Band, we also played "Hail Varsity," "Manhattan Beach," "Invercargill" and "God Bless America." Our Fairbury twirlers joined with 300 baton twirlers that performed simultaneously along the sidelines as part of the half-time show. They saluted at attention during the national anthem. Of course, I didn't view the football field from the stands, but I can imagine it looked like a giant patchwork quilt. Each band must have stood out in their unique uniforms of varied colors, forming one square of the quilt.

Band Day became so popular that it became a two-year then a three-year rotational invitation system, to guarantee at least one chance for each student to attend once during high school. The highlight was playing with the University of Nebraska Band and all the other bands on the football field. It was an unbelievable experience to be a part of that mass of color, motion and sound.

After the game, I boarded our bus with the other band members. (I made sure I found an empty seat before settling in.) My mind was filled with thoughts of my long and exhilarating day. What a feeling of satisfaction! That day left me with memories to last a lifetime.

Lois Poppe

THE NEBRASKA UNION

Welcomes You To

TOUCHDOWN BUFFET

BARBECUED SPARE RIBS
SOUTHERN FRIED CHICKEN
AU GRATIN POTATOES — BUTTERED PEAS
TOSSED SALAD WITH CHOICE OF DRESSINGS
ASSORTED MOLDED SALADS
ASSORTED RELISHES
ROLLS AND BUTTER
APPLE PIE — STRAWBERRY CHIFFON PIE
CHOICE OF BEVERAGE

Pan American Room Serving from 11:30 a.m. to 1:30 p.m.
LOCATED AT 14 & "S" ST. — FREE PARKING
Adult $1.65 Children's $1.00
Cafeteria service from 11 a.m. to 1:30 p.m. for lunch
"Crib" open all day — servicing grill and fountain orders

CAMPUS
SILVER NEBRASKA 25 UNION ANNIVERSARY
FACULTY STUDENTS
COMMUNITY

After the Game Coffee Hour . . . Main Lounge . . . Be Our Guest

NEBRASKA MEMORIAL STADIUM

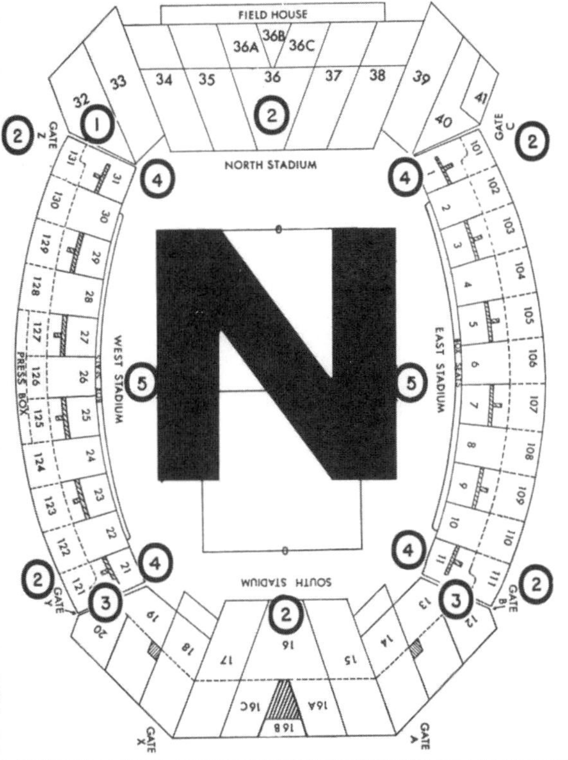

① EMERGENCIES
A First Aid Station, manned by volunteers of the American Red Cross, is located under the west side of the north stadium. Red Cross personnel are also located throughout the four stadiums.

② REST ROOMS
Men's and Ladies' rest rooms are located beneath all four stadiums, at the north and south ends in the upper levels of the east and west concourses, and at the ends of the balconies.

③ LOST ARTICLES
Articles found should be turned over to the Lost and Found offices located at the south ends of the East and West Stadiums. Persons seeking to recover lost articles after the game should inquire at the Campus Security Office, located in the Forburger building just north of the Field House. On the Monday following the game, all lost articles are taken to the University Lost and Found Dept., located at Nebraska Hall 112, 901 N. 17th, telephone: 472-2532.

④ PUBLIC TELEPHONES
Public telephones are located on the ground level under each of the four stadiums.

⑤ CONCESSIONS
Refreshment stands are located in the east and west concourse and under the North and South Stadiums; vendors circulate throughout the stadium before and during the game.

The possession or consumption of alcoholic beverages in the University of Nebraska stadium is expressly prohibited by University regulations.

Highway traffic will be heavy on all roads after the game. Please drive carefully.

"Country-Clubbed" (or, "Express" Leaves Home Without Us)

I am jazzed about getting to write an article about a Big Red memory, although I do approach all of this with a bit of trepidation, and along with the angst, a humble prayer that the statute of limitations has run out on the little caper that I'm about to unravel.

Prior to Nebraska home games, the Country Club of Lincoln has, for decades, provided bus service to and from Memorial Stadium from their clubhouse in south Lincoln. Naturally, the service was and is, for the exclusive use of their members only, and provided free of charge.

We live a mere three blocks from the Club, and one fine day, decades ago, it dawned on me, that we could perhaps walk to the bus loading area, and just sort of blend in with the club members, especially since tickets weren't involved or any other type of unnecessary hindrance! All in all, it seemed like a slam dunk. (Oops!-Wrong sport).

Then too, since my parents had been members for many years prior to moving to Scottsdale, I thought maybe I could trade on their fine name, if I indeed, was apprehended.

Well the gig lasted for about 3-plus years, with no problems at all. We enjoyed chatting with the parents of many of my friends, and we very much appreciated the door-to-door service.

Then, in the early 90s, this privileged Nirvana came crashing down, in a most-embarrassing way. Accompanied by fellow football aficionados and good buds, Bob and Sheila Warkow, Peg and I foraged our way up the hill to the Club and casually boarded the Big Red Express. No prob, whatsoever.

Then out of nowhere, a club employee began gathering some sort of ticket, or boarding pass that'd been issued from the Club. Oh, my gosh! What nerve! How dare they not trust all of us fine people! What was the world coming to?

When it was our turn to produce the transit ducats, the cupboard was bare, so I immediately invoked my fallback plan of trotting out how my parents had been members in good standing throughout the 50s and 60s and then "Oh yes; by the way, they were currently members of the Paradise Valley Country Club in Scottsdale, Arizona; a club which had reciprocal agreement with the Lincoln Country Club regarding "member privileges et-cetera!". There! That'll show 'em!

For some strange reason, none of this bluster passed muster and, (in front of many of my parent's long-time Lincoln friends), the four of us were figuratively and almost physically, tossed off the bus. Oh, the indignity of it all! Who in the thunder do they think we are?

What we were, amounted to four freeloaders, done in by a plan that me, myself and I hatched years prior, and my undoing was, well, overdue. My embarrassment rendered a face that was redder than Little Red himself, although the lesson was learned well, as we now take the Big Red shuttle that emanates out of the South Pointe parking lot. The peace of mind is well worth it; not to mention the satisfaction of an ego that has been lowered back to its proper locale.

So! As the saying goes, "All good things must come to an end", although my short-lived freebie probably wasn't all that good of a thing in the first place.

Go Big Red!

Bob Ammon

Follow The Cornhuskers

WITH

DICK PERRY

U of N FOOTBALL
RADIO PLAY-BY-PLAY
AT HOME AND *AWAY*

Broadcast with Pride by these Nebraska Radio Stations:

KCOW, Alliance	1400 KC	**KHUB,** Fremont	1340 KC	**KNCY,** Nebraska City	1600 KC	**KOLT,** Scottsbluff	1320 KC
KWBE, Beatrice	1450 KC	**KMMJ,** Grand Island	750 KC	**WJAG,** Norfolk	780 KC	**KSID,** Sidney	1340 KC
KCNI, Broken Bow	1280 KC	**KGFW,** Kearney	1340 KC	**KODY,** North Platte	1240 KC	**KRFS,** Superior	1600 KC
KCSR, Chadron	610 KC	**KFOR,** Lincoln	1240 KC	**KOGA,** Ogallala	930 KC	**KVSH,** Valentine	940 KC
KGMT, Fairbury	1310 KC	**KBRL,** McCook	1300 KC	**KBRX,** O'Neill	1350 KC	**KAWL,** York	1370 KC
KTNC, Falls City	1230 KC						

NEBRASKA
VISITORS
DOWN TO GO
FIELD HOUSE

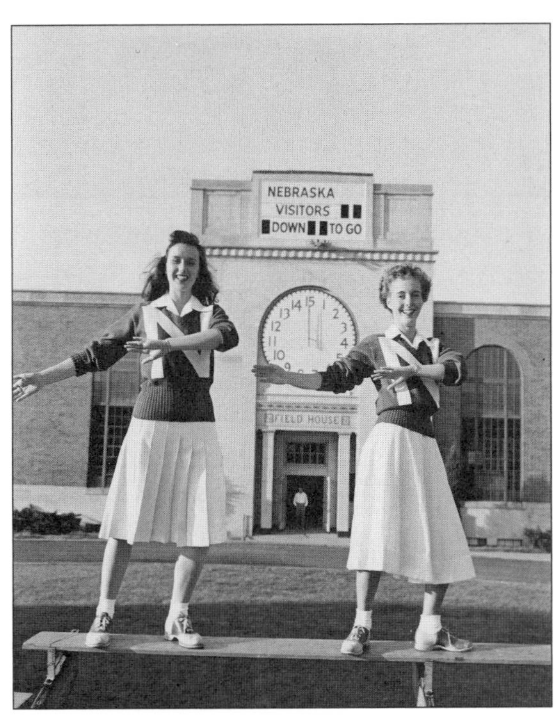

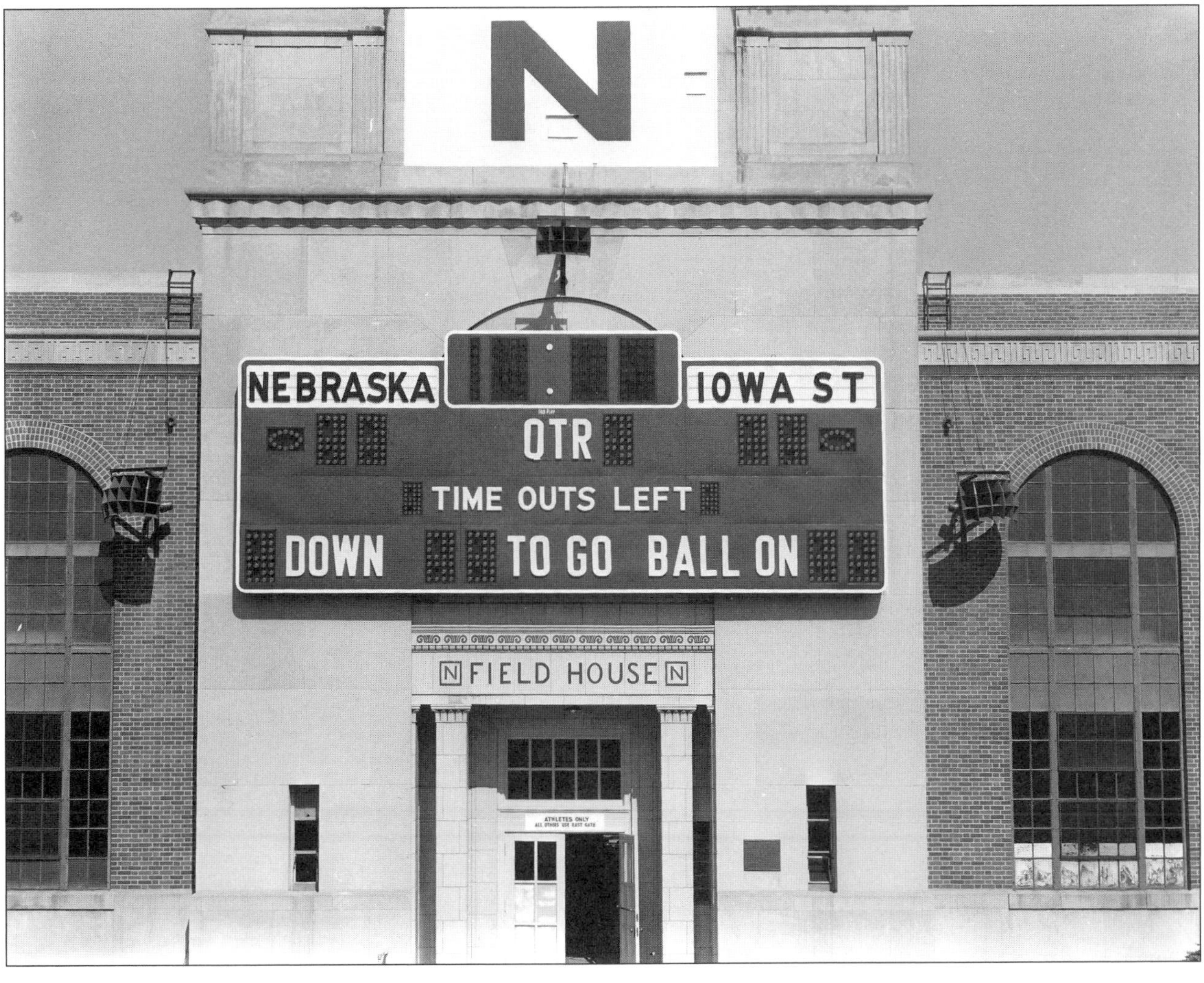
N
NEBRASKA
IOWA ST
QTR
TIME OUTS LEFT
DOWN TO GO BALL ON
N FIELD HOUSE N
ATHLETES ONLY

Ushering In A Bygone Era

"Membership has its privileges" goes the credit card slogan. For Cornhusker Council Boy Scout members of a certain rank, that meant being an usher at Nebraska football games.

In the mid-60s, you had to hold at least the rank of Star, or be an adult leader to usher at Husker games. I had just earned the Star rank in late summer of 1966, and my Troop 12 Scoutmaster, Jack Lemon, asked me if I'd like to join him as an usher that season. It would be just the two of us that year, since I was the only member of that rank that wasn't busy with a part-time job, or other diversions like sports on Saturdays.

We went to an orientation meeting at the stadium prior to the season that would train us in our responsibilities. After a briefing in the east stadium, everyone who had ushered in the past was asked to go to their section from the previous season. From that point, sections without enough people to staff them would be filled out with the newbies. Mr. Lemon disappeared to the north stadium. When they came to me, I was dispatched to section 7 in the east stadium, which looked like a prime location to watch some good football. I gathered with the group at section 7, and we got our plans in place for the opening game. A certain gate at the south end of the stadium would be open for us at noon, and with our proper usher ID, we were admitted. We then reported to our section, and four of us manned the area, spread out to cover spots where people would walk into the section. We were required to stand from the time we first reported, until the end of the first quarter. Our main job was showing people to their seats, and giving any additional help to anyone who needed it. First aid was handled by Red Cross volunteers, so we knew where they were located.

That first Saturday, Mr. Lemon picked me up in his trusty white Olds Vista-Cruiser, and we were off. That was my first real experience dealing with football traffic. He knew good spots to park, but we always walked a long way. Once settled into the stadium in my assigned section, I was ready to assist. It didn't take long to realize something about section 7. For the most part, the people in that section had been in the same one for years, and they didn't seem to need any help finding their seats. I had studied the section enough in training to be able to assist, but certainly did little of that during my time. I suppose if you were in a newer section, or the one that was sold to the visiting team, you would have had a lot more requests. Our section seemed to all know one another, longtime season ticket holders, and friends.

After the game, another requirement was for us to inspect the section for anything mistakenly left behind. Now that did require my services - because we would regularly turn up items that needed to be sent to lost and found. Nothing too valuable like a purse, but the occasional thermos, or pair of binoculars was found. And lots of popcorn boxes, drink cups, and the like. We didn't do any of the cleanup, but any large piles needed to be looked through for lost items. After about 15 minutes, Mr. Lemon would appear and we would be off to find his car. It was a pleasurable way for a youngster to see the game, and provide some service. I ended up ushering for three years, and really enjoyed it. During that time we had a few medical emergencies, where the Red Cross people came in, but nothing major. There were some elderly folks in section 7, and on occasion, a hot early season game wouldn't quite agree with them.

I have to admit, during those three years; I don't think I showed more than a couple of people to their seats. Most of them knew exactly where they were going. But, when at Memorial Stadium as an adult, if I see an usher eager to find my seat, I gladly turn my tickets over to them, and let them handle it!

Don Workman

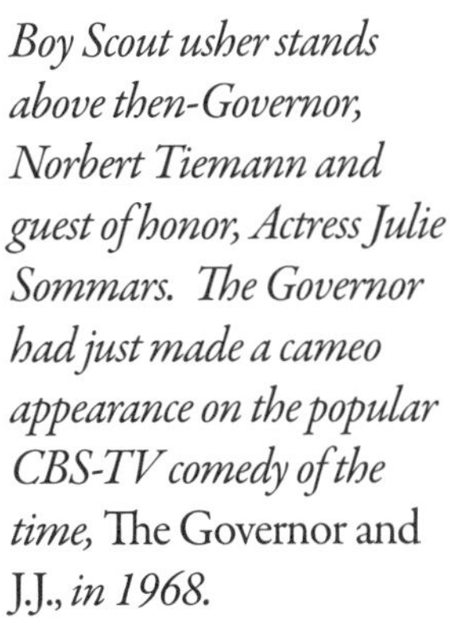

Boy Scout usher stands above then-Governor, Norbert Tiemann and guest of honor, Actress Julie Sommars. The Governor had just made a cameo appearance on the popular CBS-TV comedy of the time, The Governor and J.J.*, in 1968.*

N

29

My Exciting Trip to a Nebraska Football Game

On a beautiful, cold and crisp fall morning the conditions were ideal to travel with friends in a four seated Cessna airplane to Minnesota to attend a Nebraska-Minnesota football game in the late 1960's.

Two hours later the wind speed was 60 miles an hour or more and the vision was near zero. The wind was so bad it was tossing us around and I bumped my head. This went on for 30 minutes. We knew we were low on fuel – 30 minutes of fuel at the most. Actually we were lost. The pilot told everybody we were going down probably in a cornfield.

We were headed for the Minneapolis Airport, but couldn't make contact because of the weather conditions. And, not knowing where we were at, we were scared.

As we broke through the fog 50 feet above the ground, much to our delight and later dismay, we were lined up with the airport runway. We had no more hit the runway when the airport authority truck came with its red light flashing and they were very angry because we didn't get permission to land our plane. They measured our tanks to see if we actually had an emergency. What they found was 10 minutes of fuel remaining so no ticket was issued to the pilot.

We asked what the name of the town was where we landed. It was Bloomington, Minnesota, and only minutes away from the football game. The weather was good. We caught a taxi and went to the game. The quarterback was Dennis Claridge. In fact, Dennis threw the winning touchdown pass with sixty seconds left in the game.

This was one exciting trip to a Nebraska Football game. We stayed overnight and were thankful for the good weather on our trip home.

Lavern Priest

Football Memories

The years between 1950 and 1980 were the decades of NU football for me. I dated a guy that went to NU. After Korea, he came to the U to get his engineering degree on the G.I. Bill. I always thought of him as a kind-of older brother. I would tool down from Omaha and we'd go to the game, have dinner, and I'd tool back to Omaha. We didn't do that every game-we weren't that into football as a way of life-it was just a neat excuse to see each other. And something my Victorian MOTHER would let me do.

Once I stayed over night at the Lindell Hotel. When the guy saw me to my hotel room door, the night manager accompanied us and waited while we said our brief goodnight at the door, then accompanied him back downstairs. Ah, football memories!

Those were the days of Highway 6, not Interstate. So the road between Omaha and Lincoln was pretty much bumper-to-bumper. (I called it the sixty-mile-long parking lot.) And cars weren't that swift-at least my little 1940s green Plymouth coupe wasn't!

We soon went our separate ways, the guy and I, although he called and said how heartbroken he was when I, in 1958, married the man of my dreams. He also told all our friends that he would never be able to marry, because I had spoiled him for any other woman, and had broken his heart. (He must have thought I was a peacock, when in reality I was just a brown wren!)

In about 1956, I started dating that man of my dreams, and included in the package were FOOTBALL TICKETS. Thus began a 25-year tradition of attending all home games in Lincoln, a few assorted away games, and especially four spectacular away-game treks.

Laird and I and another Omaha couple always came to the games. We alternated food and driving-one couple drove, the other couple brought the food.

The tailgate party was always the same: pastrami and Swiss sandwiches on dark rye, kosher half-dill pickles made by yours truly every year, baked beans (very specially made with crumbled ginger snaps), brownies made from a box which we embellished, and coffee (which coffee we carried into the stadium on very cold days. Al, the guy who sat on the other side of me, always called me "Mrs. Olson" because I always had my thermos of coffee, and 4 cups!)

We even brought silver candlesticks and china, and a table cloth for our tailgate.

In those days, we really dressed for the games. We even had the white-carnation-red-pipe-cleaner-"N" corsage. It was VERY SPECIAL. When it all started, we had small children, some still in diapers, and on formula…so leaving home for a day was HUGE-baby sitter, meal preparation for home as well as the tail gate affair, plenty of formula, laundry all done, pet care arranged, perfect makeup and attire, list of emergency phone numbers, list of what to do for each child…you know! Lots of work to get ready to go. And the whole morning getting to Lincoln, especially before the interstate. The game, dinner afterward, often with other Phi Delts, and the trip back to Omaha in the dark.

Homecoming was not-to-be-missed: The Oklahoma game, Thanksgiving game, the Queen of Ak-Sar-Ben and her entourage—"Let me use the glasses to see what she's wearing!"

We parked right across from the west stadium, in a vacant lot owned by Sapp Bros., until they built the parking garage and the Champions Club. We sat in the 37th row, west stadium, under the overhang. Mary Jo and Will on one side of the 50-yard line, Laird and I on the other. Down the row from us were the Van Brunts. In those days the stadium was small enough that when Win Van Brunt shouted, "Get the ball, Nebraska!" everybody heard it.

This went on till Laird died in 1980.

In 1963, Laird and I joined several other couples on the 1890s Cornhusker Club Car to go to an away game. The Club Car was owned by Bill Kratville, whom I had known at Benson High School in Omaha. Bill could, and did, arrange with Union Pacific Railroad to attach his car to the end of UP trains going to various cities near Nebraska away games. Bill also arranged for us to have bus service to the hotel we stayed in (he also made THOSE arrangements) and for the game tickets. He was, and still is, an energetic guy.

In all, we went to the Air Force Academy in Colorado, to Kansas City, and to Minneapolis. Those years were from 1963-66. We were living in Omaha, and would pack up our clothing (especially our carefully-planned game attire!), a lunch for on the train, plus many times we took golf clubs. We would drive across the Missouri River Bridge to Council Bluffs where the Union Pacific Rail Yards were located. We'd get on the train and away we'd go for the wonderful weekend of football with friends. Snowball fights in Colorado. Friendly "congratulations" from KU fans if we won, friendly congratulations for NU fans if they won. Ice sculptures in Minnesota.

Those were the days.

I drove to Omaha one Tuesday in August 2010, to visit the train car... it is at the Western Heritage Museum, located in the old Union Pacific Railroad Station (Oh, the memories attached to THAT station–but that's another story) on the tracks beneath. Given by the Kratville family, and open to the public, it is a reminder to us of the olden Golden days when the Union Pacific Railroad WAS the way to go. Many trips to California and back I made as a young single woman. That ALSO is another story.

I no longer go to the football games, except occasionally. Husband Ted goes often. I have to go once a year for THE HOTDOG, and to carry home THE PROGRAM. Air conditioning, televised coverage and not hunting for parking have spoiled me. And I can yell and scream all I want without embarrassing my neighbors or my husband.

GO BIG RED!

Muffy Vrana

P. S. I KNOW you are wondering what happened to those wonderful football tickets. They were never ours. They were Will's. His stepfather, Julie Dralik got them as a gift from Ad Lewandowski when Ad was Athletic Director at the U. Julie was manager of the Paxton Hotel in downtown Omaha, and would comp the U when dignitaries visited Lincoln since they probably either flew in to Omaha anyway or came by train, and wanted to enjoy The City for a couple days and nights before departing Nebraska. Julie was not a sports fan, so he gave them to Will who was an absolute NUT about any sport, especially Big Red football even betting was in his DNA! So when Laird died, Will still owned the tickets, and used them for special clients of his.

Ted and I just get tickets on an "as needed" basis.

Chapter Eight

Game Day Reaches New Heights

Football Saturdays

It's 1970. Picture this: It's a beautiful Fall day in Lincoln; a Sunday afternoon and we're at the Lincoln Municipal Airport, waiting for our football team to arrive.

We had played Southern Cal the day before and tied them 21-21. We didn't know it then, but we were on our way to a national championship. By then, we knew Bob Devaney was the real deal. I think some of us thought he could walk on water. Anyway, we were kept behind the gates until the plane came in and came to a stop. We were then turned loose and could go out on the tarmac right to the plane.

The steps lowered and here came the team: Johnny R., Jerry Tagge, Jeff Kinney, Rich Glover, Larry Jacobson—and the crowd was cheering wildly. My husband and I and our three boys were very close to them as they got off the plane and began signing autographs.

And, oh my goodness, here comes Bob Devaney. People were mobbing him, but my exuberant husband went right up to him and kissed him on the cheek! As Devaney turned around with a withering look, he then started to laugh and said, "Well, hi, Sarge!" My husband was on the police department then and Devaney knew him from encounters with various team members. The coach went on to sign autographs and when he started to leave, he turned around and said to my husband, "Thanks for the smooch, Sarge!" Everybody laughed.

During the early years of the '60's and '70's, security at the football games wasn't real tight, so that gave all of the young guys a chance to try to sneak into the game by scaling walls and fences. Of course, one of the policemen would see it and try to stop them, but to no avail. As most of them made it on over, the crowd standing around that area were cheering them on!

Over 40 years ago, I had the opportunity to buy four season tickets and still have them today. I don't remember how much they were back then; I only know we didn't have that much cash lying around, so I borrowed the money from my life insurance policy–yes, I really did that! Had to pay it back over time, but I had to have those tickets! From then on, I saved back some money all year long to keep purchasing them every year.

The whole buildup to the football Saturday was trying to find parking or have someone take you down to the stadium and call for you after. Most of the time, we stopped at the band building to listen to the mini-concert they played outdoors for the fans. That put you in the mood right there! Then down to the stadium we'd go to have a hot dog slathered with mustard and a drink. We stood around and just watched the people. We sit in row 70 in the South stadium: we have a lot of ramps to climb.

And there it is; an awesome sight. You get to the top and 80,000 people in red are all there; all kinds of activities going on and you begin to smile…and everyone smiles back as you take your seats. All kinds of folks; young, old, disabled and yes, blind. There was a man there who had a companion by the arm with his white-tipped cane and dark glasses. He was there every week. At first I found that odd, but then you think about it, it's probably like listening to it on the radio. He gets the excitement of the crowd and the smells too (like Runzas, Val's and popcorn), plus the vendors calling out their various brands of pop.

I know that every team and university think they're the best; they aren't. We are. For years we've led the nation in athletes with high academics—it says that right on the stadium signage. We've had two of the greatest coaches ever in Devaney and Osborne. Frankie wasn't great, but he was good. Except for that Callahan fiasco (who, by the way, ruined many of our records except for the one he couldn't ruin: a sold-out house every week). It will be interesting to see us compete in the Big 10. Pelini will have a lot on his plate but I know he can coach his team to greatness.

So wherever we go, we will always have this feeling of "There is no place like Nebraska"!

Joyce Lattimer

Nebraska Stadium and Field House

Do you know that right before your eyes lies the best football field in America encircled by one of the finest running tracks in the world? The thick velvety sod of the field lies over a natural bank of fine sand. This layer of sand absorbs the moisture as fast as it falls with the result that the turf is just as fast in a rain storm as it is on the balmiest day in June.

The quarter mile track of red cinders, two foot in depth, built of reburnt ash is the only one of it's kind in existence. Other cinders stick to the shoes when wet but this red ash is a substance that will not track but still has plenty of life on the wettest day. Do you know that beneath this stadium built by loyal Cornhuskers there are dressing rooms, running tracks for winter work, print shops, carpenter shops, offices and training rooms?

Have you visited the new Field House with its six big basketball floors, handball courts, gymnasium equipment, tennis courts, locker rooms, showers, offices, check rooms, public rest rooms and the "N" Club Trophy Room? Fifteen hundred couples can dance on the floor at one time, eight thousand can watch a basketball game and twelve thousand can see an entertainment enacted upon the mammoth stage. This furnishes unusual facilities for both students and public.

Were you aware of the fact that this great building was built by the Athletic Department of the University from the proceeds of football games?

Take an invoice of Nebraska with this magnificent athletic plant costing well over a million dollars, with its efficient staff of coaches directed by a far seeing athletic board, and its new intramural program that will touch every student. Then decide how Nebraska ranks in athletics with other schools in America. What a fitting home for Cornhusker teams with their traditional spirit and their loyal student backing. What better could be said of a man than "He is a Nebraska Man?"

Husker Game Day Memories

Like any young Lincoln boy growing up in the 60s, I longed to attend a Husker football game. My father often worked Saturdays, and this made it difficult to go. My uncle had season tickets, and once or twice a year my father would end up finding a way to attend, while I was left at home to imitate my heroes on my field, otherwise known as my family's home in northeast Lincoln.

Over the years, both me and my friends managed to scrounge up shoulder pads and helmets so we at least looked like players. The players of the time had football pants which ended at the knee, and that, combined with the short socks they wore, often left their ankles exposed. Not to be outdone, we'd roll up our jeans to look similar. On more than one occasion, I stole the flour from mom's kitchen so we could mark out yardlines on our makeshift field.

Finally when I was about nine years old, my dad announced he was taking me to a Husker game! I was pretty much on cloud nine that entire week. Just before lunch that Friday, dad and I departed for downtown in our Husker gear. It never really dawned on me that it was Friday and not Saturday, all I knew was I was headed to see Nebraska in action!

We arrive at the stadium, and it's basically empty. But on the field are the Huskers, and their opponent. The scene was obviously not what I expected, given what I had seen on television, in the newspapers and listening to Lyle Bremser on the radio. The game began, and it mattered little that I was surrounded by empty seats. I was with my dad and the Huskers were playing! I don't remember who won, but I was still a happy camper. It wasn't until sometime later that I learned this wasn't a "real" Nebraska game, but rather the freshman team, who routinely played a few games each season on Friday afternoons.

While in junior high in the mid-70's, my friends and I would often hop on the bus and head downtown on gamedays. We'd soak up the atmosphere, eat lunch, and do a lot of walking around. Sometimes we'd visit the capitol and check out the stadium from the observation deck, which was (and still is) quite a sight. Other times we would head down to the stadium at halftime, and they'd open the gates shortly thereafter. We'd go into the stadium and prowl around, having the boy scout ushers chase us off stairs. Sometimes during the blowouts you could find an empty seat and enjoy the remainder of the game.

As time went on, my uncle's sons grew up and moved away from Lincoln. He'd call me often on Saturday mornings and offer a ticket. The cold weather games really stick in your mind. There is nothing quite like the feeling of freezing your tail off and then hopping on the nice warm bus for the ride home where usually a bowl of hot soup awaited. I sat with my uncle more times than I can remember through games in the early 80's until the mid 1990's before he eventually moved away to be with his children.

As I've gotten older, I'm not as gung-ho to go to games as before. I almost prefer the ease of watching on television, not fighting the crowds, being scrunched into a seat. But I still go every few years.

Jeff Buss

Memories of the Knothole Section

Admittedly, after 52 years the memories aren't totally clear anymore. But I remember the excitement when in 5th grade knothole cards were passed out to us before the first game of the year. It was 1958 and neither my best friend nor I had ever been to a University of Nebraska football game. Since freshmen weren't eligible then, it was also the first varsity game for someone destined to become very famous, Pat Fischer.

Of course I remember it a bit more dramatic, but, he returned a punt for a touchdown in his very first game, and Nebraska went on to defeat Penn State 14-7. Penn State finished 6-3-1 that year while NU went 3-7 under Bill Jennings. I also saw Iowa State and Kansas State play that year and in November another eastern team came to town. Like Penn State, Pittsburgh also lost by a similar score of 14-6. The 7-6 win over the Cyclones made it a typical year for the Cornhuskers.

In 1959, still in the south bleacher Knothole seats, I was there for one of the major victories of the Jennings era, the Halloween 25-21 win over Oklahoma. While that wasn't a vintage year for Bud Wilkinson's Sooners, it did end their 75 game conference winning streak. LeRoy Zentic scored on a poor punt coming right toward our bleachers. Another highlight was Jennings's idea to use 2 quarterbacks under center against Texas to open the year. With Fischer and, was it Harry Tolly (?), both behind the center the Huskers ran one series before the officials said it wasn't legal and put a stop to it. The concept was to confuse the defense since they wouldn't know where the ball was when the tandem QBs rolled to opposite sides. As with most everything that day, it didn't work, and the final was 20-0 Texas. Again the year closed with a 4-6 record but once again a Jennings-coached huge upset.

In 1961 the upset victim was Army in Lincoln. One game I attended and unfortunately do not remember any details was against Syracuse, which featured the first black Heisman winner that year in Ernie Davis.

From that point on as the Devaney era began it seems I went to fewer games for a few years. In 1963 I saw Gale Sayers 99 yard run from the south end. If I recall correctly it followed a punt that rolled dead at the 1, and drew huge cheers. Those cheers were quickly silenced as Sayers took the ball around left end and into the north end zone. Then in 1964 with the team winning on a regular basis, the stadium was expanded with the bleachers removed, the south end closed in with the first permanent expansion, and I believe that spelled the end of the Knot hole section.

Fred Hall

Memories of November 23, 1963

Almost everyone over 50 remembers where they were when President Kennedy was assassinated on November 22, 1963. It was Friday afternoon, and I, along with several of my Sigma Alpha Epsilon fraternity brothers, was at the University print shop in the old Elgin building. Our job was to prepare the programs for Saturday's football game with Oklahoma. The winner would win the Big 8 championship, and, more importantly, go to the Orange Bowl. Because of the tragedy, Friday's planned pep rally was cancelled. On Thursday, however a spontaneous snake dance started on fraternity and sorority row. Led by some Greek pep band members playing "There Is No Place Like Nebraska", students rolled out of the dorms, fraternities and sororities to join the celebration. The students, now numbering in the hundreds, proceeded south down 16th Street and then west on "O" Street, stopping all traffic as they weaved in and out of the stopped cars. The crowd ended up on the south side of the Nebraska Union continuing to sing and shout "Go Big Red". All college football games were cancelled for that weekend except two. Nebraska vs. Oklahoma was one of the two.

In fond memory of Jerry Delzell

HOME GAMES

When did I go to my first Nebraska football game? I don't know. Nebraska football has been a part of my life since I can remember. I grew up in the 1950s when Nebraska lost more games than they won, but win or lose, it sure was a great time! Our neighbors across the street had season tickets so my brother and I usually rode to the games with them. That was when tickets in the Knothole section were 50 cents. And we had a blast! We were entertained for three hours, we ate and ate, hung out with friends, and sometimes we watched the game. I remember: 1) when people got there early to hear the band and watch the team warm up; 2) the card section—that was so cool; 3) when people would carry large signs around the stadium at halftime; 4) the mascot (before Herbie Husker) was a corn cob; and 5) my brother was part of the famous "sneak in" section. The Knothole section lasted until I was in junior high. Occasionally they opened it up again if there were extra seats available. I saw my last game in the Knothole section when I was a junior in high school. I paid $5.00. Even when I was a kid the games always drew a large crowd. It was good, clean entertainment, the price was right, we were outside in the fresh air, we had a place to hang out and we saw almost every person we knew. It was just a good place to be on a crisp, fall Saturday in the 50s and early 60s.

My parents had season tickets in the 1960s and I would ride with them and hang out while they were at the game. There was a lot going on downtown and outside the stadium so it was almost as good as going to the game. Sometimes it was fun to stand outside the stadium and listen to the crowd. I remember all the stores opened early on game days. Everyone wore red and downtown Lincoln was a fun place to be on football Saturdays. Also, Miller & Paine had a fabulous lunch buffet on game days!

The Homecoming displays were so cool! Every year it was a family ritual to look at them. (I remember going to look at the displays many times on Halloween. After we were done trick or treating mom and dad loaded us in the car—we were still in our costumes—and off we'd go.) I vividly remember riding down 16th Street. Traffic was at a crawl and almost every fraternity or sorority had a display. Many of them were animated and very noisy! They had very clever displays and those kids worked hard! The display I remember the most was at the Delta Upsilon house. Nebraska played Missouri and there was a huge tiger on the roof. It was rocking back and forth and meowing very loudly. I was scared. I was back on campus the next morning for an art class and we drove by the Delta Upsilon house. That tiger didn't look so scary in the daytime!

AWAY GAMES

Kansas State

I went to three games at Kansas State. The first one was in 1965. It was memorable because my parents didn't tell us we were going to the game. They told us we were going for a drive—nothing unusual for our family. They also told us we might drive to Kansas and listen to the game on one of their radio stations, and they told us to dress up because we were going out to dinner. After we were on the road for about an hour my mother said something about how wonderful it would be if she could use magic to get four tickets. She waved her arms and said abracadabra a few times and the next thing I knew she had four tickets in her hand. I must say they pulled it off very well! My brother said he suspected something but stupid me, I knew nothing, didn't even suspect, even when mom said she was going to use magic I still didn't get it until I saw the tickets! We had a picnic lunch at a park outside Manhattan. The game was the usual 1960s K-State game. Nebraska won big. We had dinner at the Holiday Inn in Beatrice on the way home and a good time was had by all!

We went back to Kansas State in 1967. The plan was to have a picnic at the same park and eat dinner at the Holiday Inn on the way home. However, Mother Nature had other plans. It rained all the way to Manhattan so we stood at the back of the station wagon and ate in the parking lot. Our first tailgate party! The rain continued and Nebraska fumbled twice inside the 10-yard line and K-State got two quick touchdowns. K-State was ahead at halftime and the K-State fans yelled out, "WHAT'S THE SCORE, BIG RED, WHAT'S THE SCORE?" Lucky for us, Nebraska pulled it out and we won, 17-14, but it was a nail biter! In spite of everything that went wrong, we had a good time!

I went to K-State one more time in 1985. My husband and I, my brother and his girlfriend and my parents went on a bus trip. We played trivia games, my dad organized a football pool and we met some nice people so the bus ride to Manhattan just flew by. I also met the man everyone called Husker Bob. What a classy guy! It was a good trip—good weather, good game (Nebraska won), good company. We had dinner at Spike and Olly's when we got back to Lincoln.

Iowa State

Our family went to Iowa State in 1966. We had lunch at Bishops Buffet in Des Moines. All I remember was that it was a close game. Nebraska won 12-6. My mother recently told me she heard on the radio on the way home that there was a bomb planted in the field. I don't remember that. We had dinner at the Hotel Fontenelle in Omaha on the way home.

Oklahoma

We went to Oklahoma in 1968. We drove to Norman on Friday. On Saturday we met Larry Frost's parents and had a nice visit with them. They asked us if we wanted to meet Larry. Of course we did! We followed them over to the Howard Johnson where the team was getting ready to leave for the game. Larry is a very nice guy! We met some women in the parking lot at the game. They were very nice to us and wished us luck. We saw the Sooner Schooner for the first time that day. We thought it was so cute! By the fourth quarter it wasn't so cute. Unfortunately, luck—or anything else—wasn't on our side that day. Final score: OU 47, NU 0. At the time it was the worst game I ever saw! When we got back to our car we found a note on the windshield. It said, "Sorry about that! Your OU friends." If those women hadn't been so nice, we might have been offended. No hard feelings!

Baylor

My husband and I went to Baylor in 1997 on a spur-of-the-moment trip. We flew to Waco in the afternoon, went to a tailgate party, then to the game, and flew back to Omaha later that night. It was 80 degrees and sunny when we left Omaha so we were looking forward to a night game and beautiful weather. Guess again! It was cold and rainy in Waco. The bus dropped us off at the North Texas Nebraskans tailgate party. And what a party! They had three tents set up: one for food, one for beer and one with several TVs where we could watch every game that was being played that day. We had good Texas barbeque and met a lot of very nice people. It rained during the game. Baylor scored first and the stadium went crazy, but Nebraska took care of Baylor with little trouble. We tried to cover up with plastic trash bags but we mushed out and left early in the third quarter. We spent the rest of the game with our friends the North Texas Nebraskans. The flight back was very turbulent but we had a good time.

BOWL GAMES

Cotton Bowl.

The only bowl game I went to was the 1965 Cotton Bowl. I still remember where we stayed in Dallas—The Executive Inn near Love Field (before DFW). We saw where Kennedy was assassinated and also the jail where Jack Ruby shot Lee Harvey Oswald. The only marker at that time was a red circle in the window at the Texas Book Depository. I wanted to go to Nieman Marcus but they had a fire earlier that year. I did get to go to a Nieman Marcus at a shopping mall. I walked in one door, looked around a little bit and then walked out another door, but I got to say I was there! We also went to Arlington to visit some friends who used to live across the street from us in Lincoln.

The game: Nebraska vs. Arkansas. Arkansas scored first (Arkansas 3, Nebraska 0). Then we scored (Nebraska 7, Arkansas 3). The score was 7-3 for most of the game and it looked like we might win. Then Arkansas scored a touchdown. Final score: Arkansas 10, Nebraska 7. The Arkansas people were surprisingly quiet on the bus ride back to the hotel. They told us we played a good game and it could have gone either way. They couldn't have been nicer. What a classy group of people! But I did get tired of hearing SOOOO-IIII-EEEE!!

Susan McCoy

Destination: Rose Bowl

Christmas arrived early for Husker fans this year. First, Eric Crouch won the Heisman Trophy. On the following day, sports announcers made the fateful announcement. "It will be Nebraska versus Miami in the Rose Bowl!" As soon as I heard those words, I jumped into the air and exclaimed, "Yeah!" in excitement.

For as long as I can remember being a Husker fan, I've always wanted to see the Huskers play in a bowl game for the national championship. Since my friend Sarah attends the University of California at Los Angeles, home of the Rose Bowl, I knew this would be the perfect chance to go.

I'm terrified to fly and not even the chance to watch the Huskers play could lure me on to an aircraft. Being stuck on a plane for four hours at 35,000 feet just doesn't interest me. Luckily, Sarah, who was home on Christmas break, and her mom Mary Kay, agreed to drive to California with me for the game.

With the horn honking, a Husker flag flying and our excitement rising, we drove out of Omaha heading west. We were finally on our way.

Our trip to Los Angeles took over a day and a half, including some stops along the way. We slept for a few hours in the car at a rest area somewhere in New Mexico. Struggling to sleep in the front passenger seat, I woke up the next morning wondering if my body would be the same again!

On the way home, we stopped at the same rest area and saw a sign that said that poisonous snakes and insects live in the area. How comforting.

The rest of the journey to California was uneventful, yet fun. I was always on the lookout for Nebraska license plates on the highway. When we did spot fellow Husker fans, we exchanged a smile, a thumbs up sign and a wave of our red Husker flags.

When we reached our destination, we attended the pep rally on Santa Monica Pier, which overflowed with thousands of Husker fans. I got my picture taken with Lil Red and ate a Runza; it was like a small piece of Nebraska next to the beach in southern California.

After a few days of enjoying the California sunshine, it was Jan. 3, game day. As we were entering the grass parking lot, the number of Husker fans in the area was extraordinary. Cars and SUVS were lining up like offensive and defensive linemen waiting for the ball to snap.

A sense of pride in my state and favorite football team rushed through me. Cars still waiting in the street were honking their horns and even though I have seen many Husker car flags before, I couldn't help but notice and smile at the hundreds more I saw that day.

When we parked the car, I looked around and noticed that even though Husker Red outnumbered Hurricane Green immensely, that was not the case near our rental car. I grabbed the keys and moved the car into Husker territory. Let the tailgating begin.

We decided to begin by walking around and taking in the sights. Some children were tossing around a football with friends and parents. I even saw some Husker and Miami fans uniting in a game of catch. We went past the ESPN stage where the crew was busy preparing for a pre-game show that took place a few hours later.

As we were sitting around on the golf course next to the street, the flow of Husker fans into the area never slowed. Stereos were blasting the Husker fight song as fans clapped along. Husker fans dressed up as Elvis impersonators, (or Elvis impersonators dressed up as Husker fans) were the center of attention as they made their way through the crowd.

I looked around and saw a few black flags that had a red square in the middle. Feeling perplexed, I asked someone who had one on his car what the flag meant. He said simply, "Hurricane warning." Looking back, maybe I should have thought more about that warning, but at that moment, it didn't bring a sense of doom, just a smile and a roll of my eyes.

Following five hours of talking, taking pictures and eating, it was time to set aside the lawn chairs and put on our game faces. I was proudly sporting a Husker stick-on tattoo on my face and dressed in red from head to toe. We began the spirited walk from the party to the main event.

When we reached the outside of the stadium, it was a sea of red. I soon noticed, however, that this sea of red was a bit different from others I have seen before outside Memorial Stadium in Lincoln. It wasn't quiet, for screams of "Go Huskers!" could be heard from every direction, it wasn't calm, because Husker fans had been waiting 61 years to see the Cornhuskers play again in the Rose Bowl, but it was stationary.

The sea of red was actually a vast, endless line that coiled around like a snake at every corner. My watch said it was an hour before pre-game activities would start. At the rate the line was moving, it seemed like we would enter the stadium just in time to watch the highlights of next season's opening game.

While waiting in line for almost that entire hour, people in groups behind us were splitting up. One Husker fan with a cell phone ran to find another entrance, while the person left behind was anxiously awaiting the call saying he found a shorter line. Everyone was frantically searching for a way into the stadium.

I was looking back at my trip in those eternal minutes, hoping that it was not futile. A voice from the crowd broke up my moment of self-pity. I heard those magic words we were all waiting to hear, "Hey, there's no line at Gate C!"

We began to run like Eric Crouch, dodging opponents (those few Miami fans), desperately clinging to the ball (our tickets) and keeping an eye on the goal. Ok, so for those in line watching us with a dumbfounded look on their faces, shocked to see people actually get out of the line, it wasn't quite like a classic Eric Crouch run. But we all had that same determination to reach the goal, even if our goal was just to watch him get to the end zone.

At last, we made it into the Rose Bowl. I looked at my ticket, even though I memorized the seat number long ago. I went to my seat, but hardly ever sat down. I was excited to be behind the Nebraska band, but disappointed, yet again, that the only Miami fans in sight were seated by me. (I wanted to enjoy the moment surrounded by fellow Huskers.) But this time, I didn't have the choice to move, nor did I want to.

The F-16s roared overhead like thunder and contrasted against the red and orange sun-setting colors of the serene Pasadena sky. My adrenaline and Husker frenzy kicked into high gear.

Our national anthem quietly faded into the background, while Hail Varsity began to play. The Husker faithful clapped to the fight song and chanted "Go Big Red!" as our beloved team took the field.

As the football soared high into the air during the kickoff, so did my hope that the Huskers would beat Miami. It didn't take long, however, for disappointment to creep its way into my heart as the Big Red found itself falling further and further behind. The Huskers' two touchdowns late in the game raised my spirits and I found myself cheering even louder to help our chances to come back, no matter how impossible it seemed.

I watched in sadness as the time on the clock ticked down all too quickly. The chill of the January breeze settled in me, just as did the heavy realization that the Huskers wouldn't be victorious and wouldn't win the national championship…this year. I now ask the question that die-hard Husker fans ask every year at this time, how many days until the Red-White game?

Jill R. Micek
Written in January, 2001

Chapter Nine

A Changing of the Guard

FOR
YOUR
CONVENIENCE
DOWNTOWN
LINCOLN
STORES
ARE
OPEN
AFTER
THE GAME
AND YOU
CAN PARK FREE
WITH
PARK & SHOP!

S&H
GREEN STAMPS
While you're waiting
for the Interstate
to tame down...
9 We're open 'til
tonight!
Avoid the wilds of the
Interstate, the roar of traffic
by stopping in Brandeis. We're
open until 9:00 p.m. Enjoy the leisurely
comfort of dining
in our Cafeteria,
open
until
8:00 p.m.
Pick up your
weekend groceries
in our Food Basket
or shop
our
entire store
B
BRANDEIS
11th & O

Parking Cars, Pumping Gas and Poppng Popcorn

When I was a teenager I had one of the best opportunities of my life – that of learning about business from my parents. Dad was Vice President of Notifier Corporation, here in Lincoln. And Mom? A very busy homemaker. Somehow, they still found the time to operate a few businesses on the side to get us involved in learning about customer service.

One of the businesses located on North 14th Street, between P and Q, was a little ice cream and popcorn shop called the Corn Crib. It was extremely popular with downtowners and college students. On Football Saturdays it was packed with gameday-goers.

Those walking to the stadium would stop in and buy popcorn, ice cream cones, caramel corn, cheese corn, caramel apples and more, to take to the game with them. Our customers often told us we should be the official popcorn vendor in Memorial Stadium. Dad and Mom would spend the day before, as well as actual game day, working in the shop to produce the mounds of flavored popcorns, popcorn balls and caramel apples necessary to keep up with demand. It seemed like they could never be made fast enough. What fun we had when the excitement of a football Saturday filled the air in downtown Lincoln–along with that wonderful scent of freshly-popped popcorn.

Sororities and Fraternities would also get in on the action and buy our freshly made treats and take them to sell them at the stadium as fundraisers for their houses.

Right next to the Corn Crib was a Sinclair Station that my parents owned, along with two large parking lots.

While during the week downtown business people parked their vehicles in our lots, football Saturdays were a different thing altogether. On these days my dad would personally come to the station to oversee the parking situation. My Dad's way of parking cars on football Saturdays differed from the other lots around town.

Our lots accommodated a large number of out-of-towners, who trusted us to provide excellent care for their vehicles. Being just a block from campus and near downtown stores and restaurants made it the perfect place to park.

These folks came from outstate Nebraska and Iowa to see the Cornhuskers play. Like old friends, they knew where they could come to entrust their vehicle. Many told us that it was much like having a worry-free, standing reservation for their vehicle for the season.

My dad was brilliant in the way he arranged the vehicles in the lot. He squeezed them in like sardines, yet at the end of the day not one scratch could be found on any vehicle. Knowing these game-goers as well as he did, he always displayed a confidence in terms of knowing when they would be heading for home, and thus, so arranged cars for an easy exit. Customers even left their keys in the ignition, so that if it became necessary to move them, rearrangement would be a cinch. We'd watch over the vehicles from the time they arrived until the time they left for home. No tailgating at that time. Most of these car owners would be heading to one of the clubs for lunch or shopping before the game. Many used the service station's restrooms and had their vehicles gassed up and serviced while they attended the game.

My sisters and I are so thankful for our parents and all of the opportunities they gave us to work together. Then as now, we still love working and being together.

Beth Nielsen Vogel

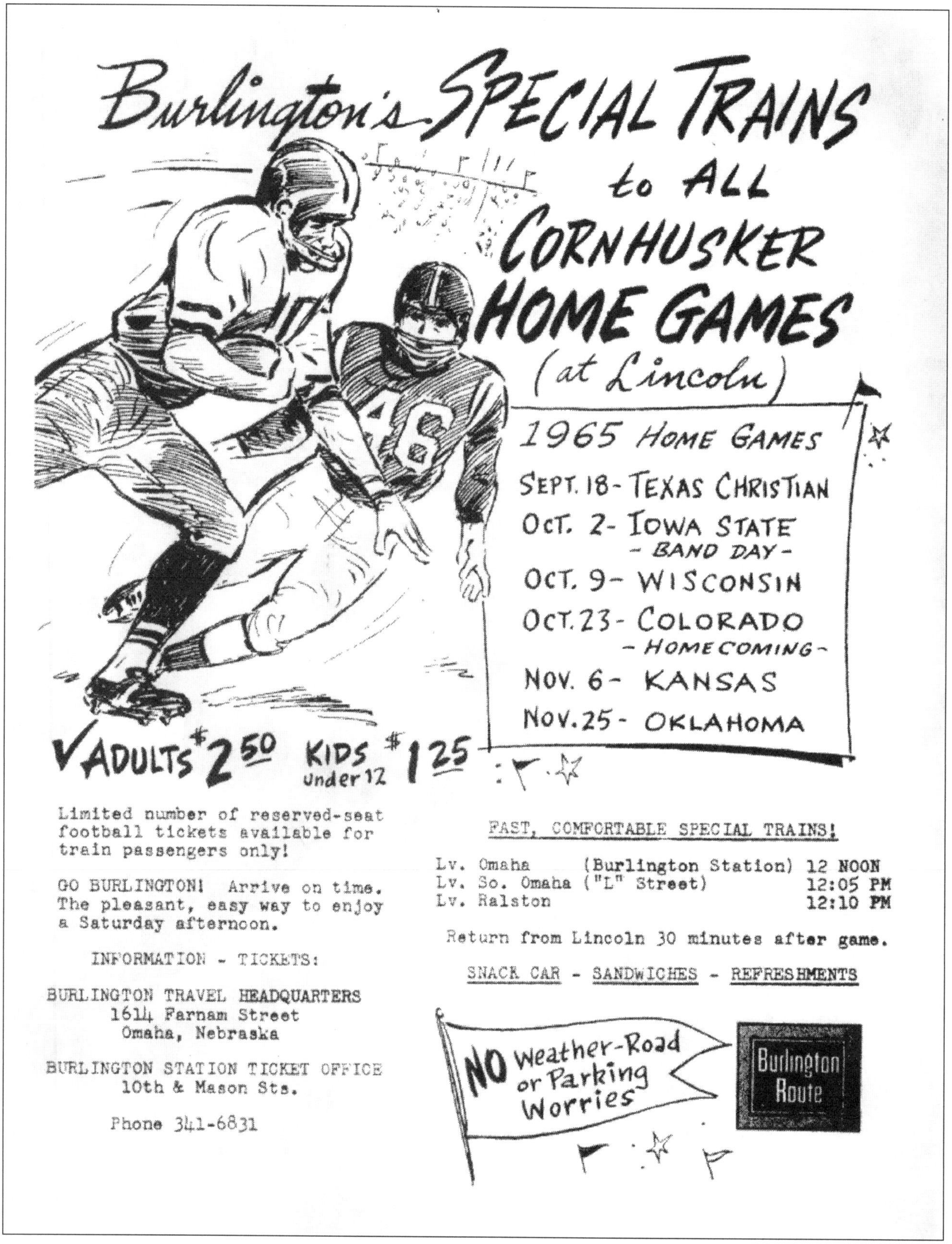

Burlington's SPECIAL TRAINS to ALL CORNHUSKER HOME GAMES (at Lincoln)

1965 HOME GAMES

SEPT. 18 - TEXAS CHRISTIAN
OCT. 2 - IOWA STATE
- BAND DAY -
OCT. 9 - WISCONSIN
OCT. 23 - COLORADO
- HOMECOMING -
NOV. 6 - KANSAS
NOV. 25 - OKLAHOMA

✓ADULTS $2.50 KIDS under 12 $1.25

Limited number of reserved-seat football tickets available for train passengers only!

GO BURLINGTON! Arrive on time. The pleasant, easy way to enjoy a Saturday afternoon.

INFORMATION - TICKETS:

BURLINGTON TRAVEL HEADQUARTERS
1614 Farnam Street
Omaha, Nebraska

BURLINGTON STATION TICKET OFFICE
10th & Mason Sts.

Phone 341-6831

FAST, COMFORTABLE SPECIAL TRAINS!

Lv. Omaha	(Burlington Station)	12 NOON
Lv. So. Omaha	("L" Street)	12:05 PM
Lv. Ralston		12:10 PM

Return from Lincoln 30 minutes after game.

SNACK CAR - SANDWICHES - REFRESHMENTS

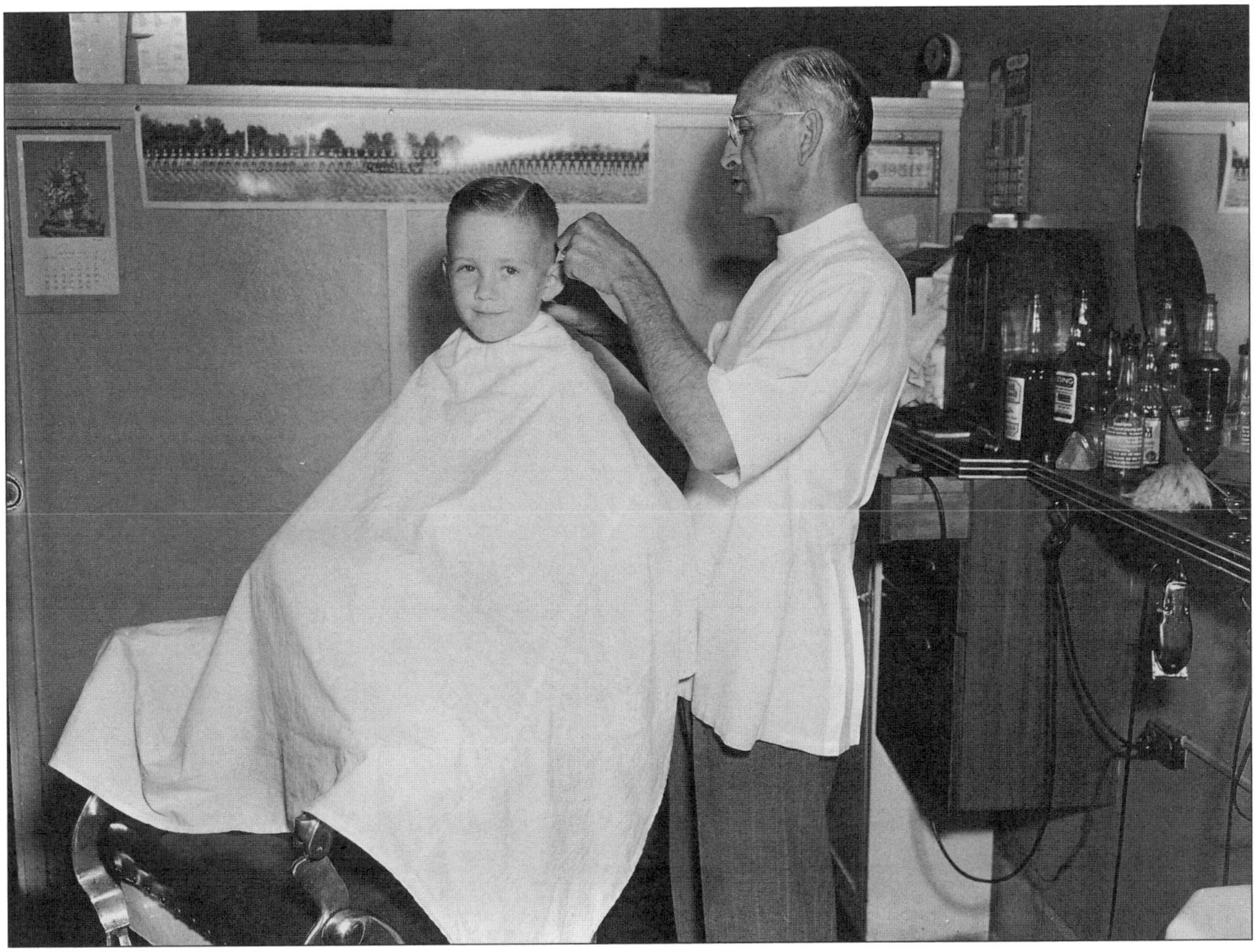

A Lasting Tribute to Photographers, Edholm & Blomgren

Whether I was headed to Odle's or the Silver Rose, I don't think there is a guy on the planet who doesn't remember one of these on the wall of their favorite barber shop. This distinct, panoramic photo of the Cornhuskers was an annual undertaking by these gifted photographers.

Today, Dick & Sue Blomgren reside comfortably at The Legacy South retirement community. Please drop them a line and let them know how much you enjoy the many photos within that help capture the spirit of all that is wonderful about Nebraska Football in particular, and the people of Nebraska, in general.

Jon Roth

My Momentary Brush with Greatness

My earliest memories of Cornhusker football were from the late 50's and into the early 60s when one of my parents would haul my brother and I along with 3-4 other kids down to Memorial Stadium in the old Dodge station wagon. They would drop us off in front of the stadium and we would pay 50 cents to sit in the knothole section. This consisted of wooden bleachers at the south end of the field. At this time this was the only seating besides the west and east stadiums as the north and south stadiums had not yet been built. We didn't worry much about wearing big red clothing to the game (I don't think there was much back then). The only thing we had to take along was a football. At halftime us kids would leave our seats and go down to the empty grass field behind the knothole section seats and get a pick-up game going. There were always plenty of kids to join us. I can remember sometimes as many as 20 on each side. As I recall we mostly played touch but sometimes it developed into tackle football. Sometimes our football game became so involved that we forgot to go back to watch the second half.

My best memory of those knothole section days was about watching the team's warm-up before the game. Back then you could leave your seat and almost get onto the playing field. The only barrier was a wooden slat roll-up snow fence about 4 feet high, which was just a few feet off the field. I remember standing just off the corner of the south end zone watching the University of Syracuse pre-game punting practice in 1961. Their kicker was at the fifty yard line and was kicking into the south end zone. One longer kick bounced over the snow fence and I managed to catch it. Syracuse Orangeman #44 came over I handed the ball back to him. All I remember him saying is" thanks kid". #44 turned out to be the 1961 Heisman trophy winner Ernie Davis.

Rick Dolen

The Identifiable Shrill of a Whistle

As any Husker fan can attest, there is a thrilling sensation from all of the sights and sounds as you near the stadium on game day. The intensity of the vehicle and pedestrian traffic mix with the sound of Hail Varsity in every concealable form and ticket hawkers on almost every corner. But, rising above those sounds is the identifiable shrill of a whistle being used by Lincoln Police officers to direct fans safely to the big game.

The familiar sight of officers in directing traffic on game days may have started in 1942. From the sketchy articles currently available, it appears that following the Husker's first appearance in a bowl game (1941 Rose Bowl, Stanford 21 - Nebraska 13), city and NU officials felt the new surge in the number of fans attending games warranted a few increased traffic control measures. Actually officers directing traffic in the 1940's and well into the 1970's in downtown Lincoln during peak times was a common assignment.

Since Memorial Stadium is on University property, the lead law enforcement agency inside the stadium is the University of Nebraska Police Department. Even by Nebraska's second bowl appearance (1955 Orange Bowl, Duke 34 – Nebraska 7), Lincoln Police officers just worked traffic and were not assigned positions inside the stadium. Bud Hynek joined the Lincoln Police Department in 1955 and remembers smaller crowds. In a recent interview he stated that officers directed traffic at just a few intersections but, did help people get across the street at N.

10th and "T" Street. Bud Hynek recalls that "we only used on duty officers for traffic assignments, there were no off duty officers used. Back then we would only send one or two officers over for the spring game". Things would soon change after Coach Devaney took his team to the 1962 Gotham Bowl and secured Nebraska's first bowl win by beating Miami. By the mid 1960's, the Husker crowds were bigger which required more officers directing traffic and were now assisting inside Memorial Stadium.

During the 1970's, parking on game day for Husker fans started to become a real problem. Retired police Sgt. Bud Hynek recalls that most people parked in the North Bottoms neighborhood and walked over the viaduct to the stadium. During one game in 1973 or 1974 some fans parked their cars too close to the railroad tracks and a train came through and hit 12-14 cars. The increase in the number of people walking over the N. 10th Street overpass and trying to cross the street by the stadium did create some interesting exchange of words. Officer Jon Morris recalls an officer directing traffic in the intersection and yells "Get up on the curb Mom!" Everyone stared at the officer who then looked at the crowd of Husker fans and says "It really is my Mom". Mom confirmed that the nice officer was her son and she promptly complied with his order. Jon Morris directed football traffic when he joined the department in 1973 and recalled that there were no surface parking lots like we have today. Fans thought, and some still do, that they can park on the sidewalk and other illegal locations on game day.

Jon remembers a car was left by its owner parked in the middle of "O" Street in front of Kuhl's Restaurant. LPD towed the car and later there was a disturbance call at Kuhl's. The owner of the car, a state senator from Wyoming, had returned and was upset that his car was missing. Typically the owner calls the police department after the game to report their car has been "stolen".

The number of officers involved in game assignments has changed over the years from just a few on-duty officers directing traffic to 70 LPD employees in the 1990's covering traffic, parking and special liquor details. Some fans believe the entire police department is mobilized for home games and fail to realize that life goes on outside of the stadium during the game. When complaints from fans stuck in traffic come in, there is little chance that officers handling calls for service in other parts of the city will be pulled to assist in football traffic.

Over the years Husker fans have walked up to Officers directing traffic in the middle of an intersection to ask every question imaginable. Some of the inquires and request for assistance have included: "Why was my car towed, What's the best way to get to Gateway Shopping mall, I think my friend has alcohol poisoning, What's the best restaurant downtown, and What was the final score"? Some fans feel the game day excitement a little too much and manage to get themselves noticed by the police for their behavior. One Saturday, an exuberant fan crossing the street,

tipped the then-mandatory police hat off the officer directing traffic. Not knowing he had chosen unwisely the now sober young man found himself in the officer's firm grip before the police hat hit the ground. He could have gotten away with his antics had he not picked Officer John Pitts, an expert in martial arts who had the young man stopped so very quickly. Officer Pitts is familiar with Husker Football having played for the Huskers as a Defensive End, Line Backer and a Monster Back. He was part of the 1970 and 1971 Husker National Championship teams and has directed traffic, rain or shine as a Lincoln Police Officer for over 30 years.

Because of their proximity to the stadium, residents of the North Bottoms neighborhood have probably seen the rise in popularity of the Big Red more than anyone else. Their concerns over parking, traffic problems, and parties have warranted extra officers being assigned to patrol that area before home games. Officer Dave Thurber remembers being assigned to assist in handling parking complaints for just that area during home games. "As I crested the top of the 10th Street Bridge heading north, I had my driver's window down since it was a warm Saturday in September. The overwhelming smell of brats and beer was in the air. A parking enforcement officer, a supervisor, and I towed illegally parked cars for almost 4 straight hours. There were also two plainclothes officers walking the same area to handle alcohol violations. As a marked unit I assisted them in giving violators a "free" ride to the Detox Center. Some people were too wrapped up in having fun and forgot their common sense."

Dave Thurber

Remembering the John Van Bloom Scoreboard

My husband and brother-in-law always bought scalpers tickets and attended the games. While they were attending the game I was usually shopping at Gateway. The one thing I truly miss is "John Van Bloom Scoreboard... and he would give the score of the teams that people called in. At the time it was a lot of teams we never played, like Wake Forrest & Tulane". It seemed like John Van Bloom Scoreboard would be on the radio when I'd get done shopping.

I remember it being dark out and either rain or snow on the pavement. It seems the show was always after dark in my memory. When I think of JVBS it takes me back to Gateway Parking lot, sitting in the car listening to the announcer. If anyone knows who the announcer was, I'd like to know. I'd give anything to hear that voice again...

Rita Schriner

Huskers Rule The World?

Back in late October 2001, my husband Virg and I spent two fantastic weeks in China! On our first full day in Beijing, Virg wore one of his favorite Husker ball caps. As we were walking down the streets along with a million or so Chinese, a young boy came up to Virg and pointed to his ball cap and said "Husker! American!"

Evie Dorn

July 4, 1947, Red Cross Motor Corps, under the direction of the Special Services Director of the Veterans Hospital, take hospitalized veterans to the tours of University of Nebraska Football games.

American Red Cross Origins

The idea of a medical emergency unit at Nebraska football games began in 1937 when the Red Cross erected a Red Cross first aid tent where the South stadium stands are now located.

In 1964 Nebraska was the first school to have a coronary care unit installed in its stadium. Fans with a history of heart problems were wired up and a radio relay sent a signal down to the aid station where their heartbeat could be read.

In 1983, the American Red Cross held it's first fund drive in Memorial Stadium to collect funds for First Aid and other services.

Today, American Red Cross First Responders work in partnership with BryanLGH Star Care Five and Lincoln Fire and Rescue to provide First Aid services.

Randall S. Jones
Chief Executive Officer
American Red Cross
Cornhusker Regional Chapter
Lincoln, Nebraska

How Sweet It Is!

On December 6, 1971, we were on a Big 8 Nebraska Alumni Tour to Hawaii, where we were playing them for the first time. This picture was taken during the game. There were so many Nebraskans in attendance that it was almost like a home game. We still attend all of the Nebraska home games.

Kep and Kay Harding

How sweet was victory for these University of Nebraska Cornhusker fans in Hawaii for the football game?

Sporting a "How Sweet It Is" poncho is Mrs. John Bottorff. Others are (from left) Mr. Bottorff, and Mr & Mrs. Kep Harding.

Chapter Ten

Game Day Groovies

Husker Game Day

Husker game day brings to mind many images and memories. My first recollection of a memorable Nebraska game was on October 31st 1959. My brother and I were in our basement glued to the radio not believing what we were hearing. Our shouts filtered upstairs where Dad was doing his usual pacing back and forth like some expectant father in a hospital waiting room as unranked Nebraska shocked the college football world by snapping the Sooner's 74 game win streak, and 38 consecutive Big 8 conference wins by a score of 25-21. Being car less, we were unable to join the throng of fans as they paraded the goal posts down O Street. Later this trophy would get cut up into thousands of pieces and sold as souvenirs. We had one of these, but alas somewhere along the line it was lost, however, the memory remains.

One remarkable game I did attend was another classic between Nebraska and Oklahoma. Who can forget the gritty performance on November 11th 1978. Phyllis was a student at the university, and bought a student ticket for me to use. When attending games, I showed her student ID along with my ticket, and was allowed in-no questions asked. Sometimes the person checking ID's, and tearing ticket stubs would give me a funny look, or a smile. Occasionally I would hear "Enjoy the game Phyllis." Back then; Husker cowboy hats were in vogue. I took mine one-step further by flattening the brim in the fashion of the hats Clint Eastwood wore in his "spaghetti" westerns. On that crisp day, the Blackshirts forced 9 sooner fumbles. The result was that myself, and the 76,014 other fans spent more time standing, than we did sitting on our hard, gray painted, plank seats. With arms raised, shaking to and fro with clenched fists, we shouted encouragement. When I returned home, my voice sounded like I had severe case of laryngitis from constantly yelling De-fense, De-fense, De-fense. What made this victory so satisfying? It was Tom Osborn's first win over Barry Switzer, and an Oklahoma team that he said later was his best team during his tenure as OU's coach. Add to that the Sooners were #1 at the time, and as Jackie Gleason would have said, "How sweet it is." I still have my ticket stub from this game.

On September 24th, 1983 I attended the Nebraska-UCLA game. For me this game is noteworthy for one play. Some say the run by Mike Rozier on this day in front of the usual sell out red clad crowd, and a national TV audience on ABC, sealed his Heisman Trophy, even though this was only the Huskers fourth game of the season. For those who may have forgotten, Rozier brought the crowd to its feet, yelling and screaming on his seventeen-yard run. Officially it went in the record books as a two-yard touchdown. The Husker I-back started left, was hemmed in, reversed his field backward to the seventeen-yard line, swept to the right, and avoided several tacklers before crossing the goal line.

One game I wish I had attended was in 1988 against Oklahoma State. Nebraska was ranked #7, while the Cowboys came in at #10. In 1988 OSU had their version of the triplets. At quarterback was their now head coach Mike Gundy. Hart Lee Dykes was a split receiver, and at running back was the eventual Heisman Trophy winner in 1988 Barry Sanders. This game was not televised, and when it was over, I'm sure the networks wish it had been. Kickoff found Phyllis and I were doing a volkswalk on the streets and dusty, gravel road in and around Weeping Water. This for me was a difficult walk. Not from the ups and downs, or distance we walked, but because as a die-hard Husker fan, I was missing most of the game. I was able to pick up bits and pieces of the games progress from other walkers who had Walkman radios. I missed most of the scoring as Nebraska raced to a 42-0 half time lead, and hung on to win in a shootout 63-42.

I'm sure there's one thing brides in Nebraska want to avoid above all else when planning fall nuptials. Don't have your wedding and reception on the day Nebraska plays, especially if the game is at home, and on TV. In 1997, one of my coworkers had their wedding set for October 4th. They had checked in advance, and the #3 Nebraska and #17 K State game were scheduled for early afternoon. The wedding and reception time was set to follow the game, however, the powers that be had other ideas. The game was changed to nighttime to accommodate television. No problem for the weeding itself. The reception however, was another matter. So there we were atop of the downtown Rock and Roll Runza at a wedding reception, sneaking looks at every available opportunity at the TV screens showing the game. It was with much difficulty that we Husker fans at the reception tried to keep our enthusiasm in check as Nebraska went on to a 56-26 win. Neither bride nor groom being sports fans, were not happy campers.

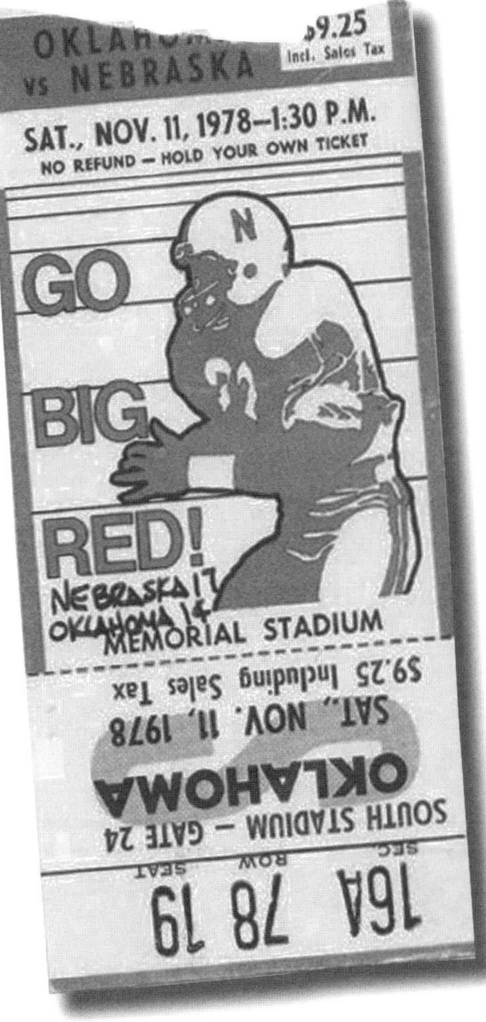

I could go on, but these are my memorable Husker game day experiences. With a few lean years behind us, and a new coaching staff on solid ground, the Huskers are back. I look forward to adding more Husker game day memories, and hopefully another national championship or two.

Go Big Red!

Les Williams

Food for Thought: The Greatest of Victories Can't Fill An Empty Stomach

My husband, Richard Schenaman, was a BIG Nebraska football fan. We had never traveled to an away game to see Nebraska play, but he decided to surprise me and bought two bus trip tickets that KFOR was selling to see Nebraska play Oklahoma on Thanksgiving day 1971. The tickets were $49 each and included round trip bus fare, game day tickets, motel room, and a box lunch on the bus.

We left Lincoln at 11 p.m. on Wednesday night and reached Norman, Oklahoma around noon on Thanksgiving Day. We had supper at home around 6 p.m. on Wednesday night. There was no sleeping on the bus that night as they had beer and soda pop, and a full bus of excited fans. We did not stop for breakfast as it was a tight schedule to make it to the game on time.

When we arrived, they gave each person a box lunch. It had chips, a sandwich and an apple. We decided to buy a hot dog at the game so I did not eat my apple. Being a trusting person and assuming we would sit in our same seats when we got back on the bus, I left my apple on the seat.

It was really cold at the game and it was a packed stadium. At half time I went to get our hot dogs. When the person handed them to me, the bags were turned upside down. When I got back to our seats, all I had in my hand were two empty bags. We laughed and thought, "oh well we'll eat when we got back to the motel."

The game was a nail-biter right up until the last few minutes, when Johnny Rodgers made the final touchdown. Nebraska won, 35 to 31. The place was wild! Oklahoma fans were not happy with us Nebraskans that day. We all hurried to our buses. When we got to the bus, our seats were taken. My apple? Long gone! Again, we said, "Oh well, we'll eat in Oklahoma City at the motel."

By now we're REALLY hungry. When we arrived in Oklahoma City, the only place open was the bar in the motel. But, NO FOOD! There were fast food places all around the motel but every one of them had closed for Thanksgiving. Not even a pop machine in the lobby to get something to drink. By this time it is after 10 p.m., and we're exhausted, so we take showers and head off to bed.

The next morning we rushed to get breakfast in the motel dining room, as we had about 20 minutes to get something to eat before the bus started for home. The dining room was packed and it was pretty obvious we wouldn't get waited on in time to meet the buse's departure. If we didn't get something to eat soon, the next time any kind of an opportunity would present itself was far away, in Kansas, later that afternoon.

We managed to find a big restaurant that still had turkey and all the fixings on their menu. That was, by far, the best-tasting Thanksgiving dinner I ever ate! I think that was the first time in my life I could ever say I was truly hungry. It was an unforgettable trip and a game I'll always remember.

I knew Bob Devaney very well and spent some time inside his office. On the walls there were pictures of himself and the team with President Nixon at the White House, pictures with Bob Hope, and pictures taken with many other celebrities. One day, we were talking and I asked Bob what the best decision of his life or career might have been. He said, "Becky, the best thing I ever did was marry my wife." That spoke volumes about the man. He had his life set with the right priorities.

He was a great coach, but he was an even nicer person.

Becky Schenaman

THE WHITE HOUSE

WASHINGTON

January 19, 1971

Dear President Soshnik:

The enthusiastic welcome w
versity of Nebraska last Th
the day a great pleasure as
We are especially grateful f
you gave us in connection wi
ments necessary, and I want
to express my appreciation t
that you did.

The beginning of a second hun
this nation's great universitie
and it was particularly exhilar
present with all of you as you
of great endeavor.

Mrs. Nixon and our daughter join me in sending you our best wishes for the future.

Sincerely,

Richard Nixon

The 1995 Nebraska Football Team – Possibly the Best Team…Ever!

Schedule and Final Scores:
8/31/1995: NU 64 – at Oklahoma State 21

09/09/1995: NU 50 – at Michigan State 10

09/16/1995: NU 77 – Arizona State 28

09/23/1995: NU 49 – Pacific 7

09/30/1995: NU 35 – Washington State 21

10/14/1995: NU 57 – Missouri 0

10/21/1995: NU 49 – Kansas State (ranked #8) 25

10/28/1995: NU 49 – at Colorado (ranked #7) 21

11/04/1995: NU 73 – Iowa State 14

11/11/1995: NU 41 – at Kansas (ranked #10) 3

11/24/1995: NU 37 – Oklahoma 0
(Final Big 8 Conference football game)

01/02/1996 – Fiesta Bowl, Tempe, AZ
National Championship Game: NU 62 – Florida (Ranked #1) 24

Average score 1995: NU 53 – Opponent 14

The Fiesta Bowl had a crowd of 79,864 in attendance. Among them, me, my wife, Beth and her immediate family. We arrived in Scottsdale a couple of days before the big game and the atmosphere was electrifying. Husker fans were everywhere. I'd have thought we were still in Nebraska except for the palm trees, mountains and weather in the 70's instead of being below zero with snow on the ground. Tons of pre-game events were going all around us, many sponsored by Tostitos. We were"tail-gating" along with numerous other Nebraska fans on New Year's Eve when my Father-in-law informed us that he had made reservations at a local restaurant. We were hesitant to leave the festivities, but in doing so ran into three ESPN "Game day" hosts (Lee Corso, Chris Fowler and Craig James) sitting at a table next to us. We chatted a bit about the Big Red and had photos taken with them...what a great time! We were, once again, impressed by our father-in-law's wisdom. We took the day "off" on New Years, went golfing and enjoyed the spectacular 70+ degree weather.

Then it was "Game-Day" - January 2nd. We all caught a ride to Tempe early in the afternoon and went to the tail-gate that was set up for the Nebraska fans just outside of the stadium. Again, Tostitos was represented everywhere. After about an hour or so of enjoying the festivities, we headed to the stadium, loaded up on some souvenir t-shirts and programs and settled in for the fun.

It was #1 Florida (also undefeated) vs. #2 Nebraska and the atmosphere was electrifying as the National Championship game got underway with the opening kickoff. Both teams traded blows and Florida was up 10-6 after the end of the quarter. Confidence was still high from the husker fans and sideline. In the 2nd quarter, that confidence changed to exuberance as Nebraska took control of the game by scoring 29 unanswered points. We led the game 35 – 10 going into the half.

The 2nd half was more of the same, with Tommie Frazier running in for one touchdown, followed by the one that most husker fans will remember forever, the one where he was stood up, then broke free for a 75 yard run, breaking at least 6 or 7 tackles along the way. It was at that moment, that I recalled yelling out to anyone that cared to listen "put a fork in it, it's over"! The score was 49 – 18 after the 3rd quarter, and the Florida coaches (lead by Steve Spurrier) and the Florida fans were in complete shock after seeing what had transpired in the 2nd and 3rd quarters. Of course, on the other side, the husker fans were ecstatic. The final score was 62 – 24, in what I read somewhere was the 2nd largest winning margin in a matchup between a #1 team vs. a #2 team. Needless to say, the Nebraska fans partied well into the night!

Russ Vogel

Football Unlimited trip to the NU-CU game in Boulder during the mid-1970s. Left to right: Kenny & Helen King; Ray & Amy Frohn; Rex, Opale & Deb Oman; Sharon & Mervall Bumgarner.

Football: A Part of Life in the Cornhusker State

For most Nebraskans, Big Red Football has unlimited possibilities. It is a year-around topic of conversation. Many fans start the next year with "the bowl game" followed by planning for the next season's home and away games and anticipating "the Spring Game" then keeping track of depth charts until Labor Day weekend and the first game of the season.

University of Nebraska football is a part of life in the Cornhusker state. It was at the heart of friendships among 11 Nebraskans from North Platte, Beaver Crossing, Lincoln and Geneva. They called themselves "Football Unlimited". However, the beginnings of this group of fans began in the early 1950s when the Cornhuskers were not a national power, much less a winning team.

Chapter Ten · *Game Day Groovies*

Fall in the '50s was simpler. Most Nebraskans "saw" Nebraska football games on the radio while doing weekend chores. In this case one weekend activity was duck hunting on the Platte River just east of North Platte. Rex Oman and his best friend Virgil Egle hosted friends to hunt from the Lincoln area that included Ray and Amy Frohn, Farley Young, Lyle and Doris Davis and a fellow named Lewandowski who was the head football coach for a short time, as well as head basketball coach, athletic director and athletic department business manager for the University of Nebraska.

Once in a while Rex would get tickets to a Nebraska game for his wife Opale and daughter Debbie (Deb) from "Lew". Those were special weekends. The Omans would meet up with Ray and Amy while in Lincoln. By the mid-1950s, the Omans and Frohns had two traditional football weekends. One for a game in Lincoln scheduled around duck hunting. The other was in October during "teacher's break" since Opale was a grade school teacher in North Platte. Back then the big game was against the Colorado Golden Buffalos. Every other year the game was in Boulder, a perfect destination for a fall trip.

Now remember, those early trips to Colorado were before the days of the Interstate System, so there were a lot of stops along the way. Paxton and Ogallala in Nebraska then Julesburg and Hudson in Colorado each had a special place to revisit. Each trip allowed plenty of time to catch up on each other's activities since the last trip. Those are the things of deep friendships.

By the mid 1960s, the Omans had Nebraska season football tickets. They left North Platte after school on Friday, drove to Lincoln and met Ray and Amy for dinner. Football Saturdays featured a little shopping at Gold's, Miller & Paine, Hovland-Swanson, Magee's and others before the game.

Others joined the Omans and Frohns for a pre-game pot-luck lunch in the backroom of Ray and Amy's downtown office. Mervall and Betty Bumgarner, Kenny and Helen King, and Bob and Norma Allen became the core for "Football Unlimited". When the Centrum block was developed, the group had to find another place for pre-game. Kenny came to the rescue by finding a vacant office in a downtown building. The group decorated a 10' x 10' room with red carpeting and second-hand furniture. Deb became the "ice chairman". Betty took charge of roast beef for sandwiches. Everyone else brought a covered dish and beverages. It was better then tail-gating since we could clean up after the game while the traffic cleared out of town.

By the mid-1970s Football unlimited was traveling to all of the Nebraska away games in the Big Eight conference. Each family volunteered to arrange lodging for the group for the "road trip". Car-pooling and caravan travel was the norm. New football friends were made at every stop. As you can image, there are many stories to be told.

For one trip to Manhattan, Mervall and Betty had a Friday commitment and needed to meet the rest of the crew there. Someone decided (probably Bob or Norma) that we should take one vehicle since we didn't have a lot of luggage. Image nine adults in a large station wagon with a rear-facing seat (no, not a van) riding for three hours from Lincoln to Manhattan. I'm sure we were quite a site cruising down the road. We laughed a lot, and no one complained, at least out loud.

Trips to Colorado had the longest history. We stayed at a Travel Lodge close to the University of Colorado campus so that we could walk to the game. We never had problems with opposing fans, probably because we made friends instead of enemies. During one particular trip, Football Unlimited had Friday evening dinner at "The Golden Buff". Kenny enjoyed a good martini from time to time. He and the manager started kidding each other from the moment we got there. Kenny's first "martini" was water with golden olives. After much cajoling and laughter, a great time was had by all. We looked forward to eating there each visit until it closed.

If the group couldn't caravan together, we all met at the chosen motel. Each arrival was an event with smiles, hugs and warm greetings. Each weekend was a celebration of Nebraska football and friendships.

Stillwater, Norman, Lawrence, Manhattan, Columbia and Ames, along with Boulder, each had fun places to visit or shop, great places to eat, beautiful campuses with rich traditions and a wonderful atmosphere for Big Eight football. Win or loose, the Football Unlimited group enjoyed their football. Post-game analysis was always lively. Discussions involved everyone. No feelings were ever hurt. After all the next weekend was another game.

By the 1990s the ranks of Football Unlimited had dwindled. Road trips were made to visit sick friends or to go to funerals. As of this writing, five of the charter members remain to cheer the Huskers- Deb, Amy, Helen, Mervall and Betty. We each have fond memories of Nebraska football trips and friends. Of course, there are stories to tell about each and about Nebraska football.

Today games are different. There seems to be more hype and commotion. Game days have lost their intimacy. Yet, the traditions are still there. The Big Eight is now the Big XII. New football friends have been made, but there will never be another group like Football Unlimited. It was special. It evolved from sharing time with friends who cared about each other and about Nebraska football. Go Big Red!

Deb Oman and Amy Frohn

*Pictured left to right:
Deb Oman, Amy Frohn and Helen King.*

A Few of My Favorite Game Day Moments

My favorite Game Day Memory is coming to Lincoln (as I lived in Holdrege, Nebraska at that time) and watching my first football game ever at Memorial Stadium. Nebraska was playing UCLA, a game in which Mark Harmon, of television fame, was quarterbacking for the Bruins. It was also Head Coach Tom Osborne's first game and the Huskers won the game, 40-13. I have many fond memories of eating some great breakfasts at Kuhl's Restaurant before the games, and then, of watching that sea of red as it sojourned to Memorial Stadium.

Karen Kammann

P. S. Another favorite Game Day Memory is going to the Cotton Bowl in Dallas and watching the Huskers lose 17-14 to Houston. (I think that was either in 1979 or 1980.)

My all-time favorite game day memory is one of going to Hawaii with my parents and girlfriend, Dolores (Borchers) Hellwege of Grand Island and going to the Aloha Bowl and watching the Huskers play the Rainbows there in December of 1982!

Husker Groupies

It began in 1991 as a joke and evolved into a tradition. Almost 20 years ago. This is the history behind it. We attended Coach George Darlington's Football 101 classes year after year. His classes were part Husker history, part football lore and part insider hints at what to watch for in the next game. It was all exciting to say the least and being devout Husker fans we couldn't get enough. Typical Husker groupies!

Coach Darlington ended each year with a banquet to celebrate another successful class and to allow the "students" to meet some of their favorite players. The players signed autographs, answered questions from the crowd and posed for pictures with class members and their guests. So back to the joke and soon-to-be tradition. Each year we would use some portion (yes, photo editing took place even back then courtesy of Diane Parks-another fan) of our picture with the players and coaches to create a Christmas card to send nationwide to colleagues. We became more creative in later years when Coach Darlington was no longer on the Husker staff. We worked in the Early Childhood and disability areas of state government so we had the opportunity to meet many people from other states. We were always able to hand out Husker football schedules as part of presentations we made at national meetings, a gesture that riled the crowd but created a lot of enthusiasm at the session. We found that people on our Christmas card list (usually 125+ cards) waited for the cards each year and questioned us if the cards did not arrive when anticipated. Some people even "collected" the cards and would display the "set" as part of their Christmas decorations.

We tried to tie each card to a theme that described the football program for the season or the atmosphere surrounding it. In 1993 with Trev Albert and Sister Barbara Ann, a former Football 101 student and St. Elizabeth Hospital staff member, we couldn't resist "Nebraska Football is a Religious Experience." We celebrated in 1996 with a picture of the two of us between the national trophies on the Husker Vision screen – "Back to Back Husker Greetings." And in 2001 we were "Remembering the Ghosts of Huskers Past" with a variation of the famous picture of Tom Osborne being carried off the field by us and "God Bless the Huskers, every one!" Little did we know how prophetic that turned out to be.

Sure people think we're crazy, but isn't that part of being a Husker fanatic? It's the culture that surrounds the Husker Nation; it's the culture that fills Memorial Stadium, win or lose. And we wouldn't want it any other way.

Jan Thelen & Mary Jo Iwan

Football 101

So many great memories on game day. Not sure what year it was, but I do remember a warm Saturday because I had red shorts and a white tank top on. Sitting in the west stadium, south end, I noticed the sky changing and told my friend that I didn't like the looks of the clouds. About three minutes later the sky opened up and we were (and, I really mean) soaked. Everyone headed under the stadium in a panic. I told my friend I am not going into that mob because we were already as wet as were going to get. The field was covered in water. Then, lightning started and they removed both teams from the field. We also went under cover at that point. About 15 minutes later everyone went back to their seats and the game resumed. Can't remember who won. It was pretty funny. I felt like I had taken a shower at Memorial Stadium.

I will always have fond memories of the Football 101 class by George Darlington. I always took these classes. He offered them several times. He was so patient and kind and really taught us women a lot about football. Because of those classes I can now talk football with the best of them. Each year we would have a class sweatshirt made exclusively for that class and that year. They gave us tours of the stadium. They took us onto the field where we would put on the numbers of the players that corresponded to a particular position and then learn, firsthand, *that* position. I remember one year I grabbed Grant Winstrom's #98 and played his position. I loved watching Grant play. The following week George would go over some the of plays with us. We had footage we watched so that we could review the plays and have George explain the calls. At the end of the class there was a banquet in which George would have two current players in attendance to talk to us.

I remember George telling us, "If Nebraska loses a game it is not the fault of the boys, but of the coaches." He said, " We're the ones who coached them wrong." That statement has always stayed fresh in my mind.

I have attended two National Championship games. One under Coach Devaney in Miami, Florida (the very first one, against, I believe, LSU), and the second in Tempe, Arizona under Coach Osborne against Florida, a game in which Tommy Frazier managed to shake off a total of nine Florida Gators and run for a touchdown. We were in the south end zone and he was running straight toward us. We were jumping, yelling and screaming so hard that I thought I might have a heart attack, my heart was beating so fast. It was a great moment and one in which most Gator fans started leaving the stadium. Needless to say, by the time the game was over, the stands looked very empty.

Nebraska is one of the best places in the world to watch college football. Memorial Stadium, the best place to be seated in on any given football Saturday. I never get tired of the band, of the Nebraska fight song or any other Husker songs for that matter. In fact, I have some loaded on my computer which I play in off-season because I miss hearing them. Especially the song "Can You Hear Me". Whenever I play it, the stadium just seems to fill right up.

Pat Holle Novak

Photo Day

Before the Nebraska Cornhuskers had what they now call "Fan Day", fans were allowed into Memorial Stadium after the preseason "Photo Day" event. There would only be a couple hundred fans there because it would be a weekday and most adults would be at work. I would take the city bus downtown and meet my Dad at his office across from the State Capitol. After eating lunch, we would walk over to the football stadium. A lot of times we would see the football team getting their panoramic team photo taken. The Huskers would all be lined up in a half circle in front of an old fashion camera on three legs. The cameraman would slowly rotate the camera from one end to the other. Soon after the players stood around the football field as their fans ran from player to player to get autographs and photos. Of course the popular players would have a dozen people around them, whereas the freshmen would have none. I would usually be able to get an autograph of all my favorite players without standing in line forever, as is the case, nowadays. I remember these Photos Days from many years ago because it was one of the few times I could get my Dad away from his work and not to have to share him with my four older sisters.

Decades later when my son Paul was born, I dreamed that he would be the football player I had not been. Starting at 8 months old, I took my son to every Nebraska Fan Day until he was attending Lincoln Southwest and had his own football practice to attend instead. Every football season I would get a special outfit and football for my son. One memorable year was when my son was five years old in 1995. Earlier, my in-laws had won an official Husker football helmet from their bank and had given it to my son. We, as usual, were among the first in line at the stadium. We decided to have only a few people sign the football helmet. My son was the first person to get Tommy Frazier's autograph. People everywhere were taking photos of him. Later, we stood in our longest line and added Coach Osborne's autograph to Frazier's on the helmet. The next morning, both the Sunday Lincoln Journal-Star and Omaha World-Herald had a color photo of Tommy Frazier signing my son Paul's football helmet. My son's face was not shown, but his little hand was. Years later, my son would play football at Memorial Stadium as a Southwest Silverhawk and is now a student manager for the Cornhusker football team. My son still prizes his Cornhusker helmet from that National Championship season over the many signed footballs which can no longer be read.

John Belz

Proof Positive: Picture-Perfect Day Doesn't Always Require Film in the Camera

The fall of 2003 brought a visit from my daughter-in-law and her grandparents from Ohio. Our plans were to visit Memorial Stadium and check out the playing field up close.

After arriving at the stadium, we wandered around and found a door leading out to the field. We had fun posing for all sorts of photos: running for a pass, cheerleading and celebrating touchdowns.

We weren't sure which door to use to head back out of the facility, and as we entered back into the interior of the stadium, we suddenly realized we were in the team locker room surrounded by several casually-dressed players who all towered over us. They smiled when Grandpa politely asked for pictures, but all granted his request very graciously. As we turned around, Coach Solich also appeared and agreed to a few pictures as well. We were all thrilled and appreciative of his kindness.

After visiting with us for a moment, Coach Solich lowered his voice and softly said, "You probably weren't aware of it when you entered, but you folks are in restricted space, designated for players only, so you should probably vacate the area as soon as possible." He then very politely showed us the way out, thanking us for our Big Red support.

It had been a perfect day full of joy and laughter and the grandparents were excited to share their adventure and pictures with their friends back home.

How did the pictures turn out? They didn't. Grandpa forgot to put film in the camera! So much kidding took place, but, as a result, the four of us had fabulous memories to share and soon discovered that we didn't need film to document our "picture-perfect" day!

Victoria Springer

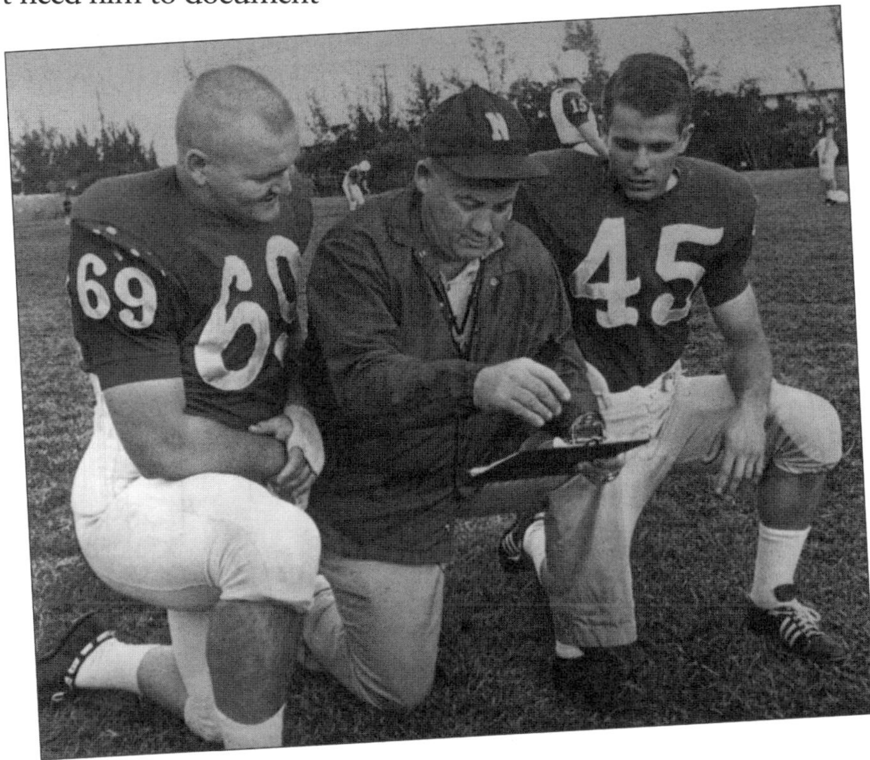

Fullback Frank Solich and Linebacker Mike Kennedy going over a few last-minute details with Coach Bob Devaney just before the Orange Bowl played in Miami, Florida on January 29th, 1965.

Something Fills the Air

There is something very special about a game day in Lincoln Nebraska. Something fills the air on these fall days – the likes of which no other day of the year will know.

For but a handful of Saturdays between August and December it seems that everything stops and the focus of an entire city and state becomes captivated and fixated on one thing... Nebraska football–and all that surrounds the day. Everything from the Tailgating to Touchdowns to Traditions... Game Day is a day unto itself.

This feeling has been with me since I was a child. I can recall football Saturdays back then as if they were just yesterday. While I did not attend games until I was eighteen, the times I spent downtown on game day greatly impacted me. I recall the streets were packed with people clad in red and white clothing -- no black clothing. And I don't recall seeing many imprinted team t-shirts, if any. Women were dressed up – in skirts, hose and heels! Many men wore red leisure jackets, white pants, red hats and white shoes! As they walked north from O Street to the stadium, they would be toting stadium seats, thermoses, and stadium blankets. All looking as comfortable and moving along as easy as we see people today in tennis shoes, jeans and sweatshirts.

Today, like then, I still enjoy hearing the rumbling of the drums, the sharp clear voice of the game announcer and the roar of cheers from the stadium. It will always be meaningful for me to look to skies above the stadium when the first score is made to see the lift off of thousands of red and white balloons celebrating all that Go Big Red stands for. And the times when I have not attended the game or a game party to watch the game, I have always loved to hear the game being played over the sound systems in the stores around town. The energy that was and is conveyed through the announcer over the radio has always made me feel to be a part of it all– even if I was not able to be in the stadium to see the game.

For over twenty-five years my Game Day friends and I have enjoyed football Saturdays together. We've enjoyed all that the day offers –before, during and after the game. And no matter if the game days are spent at Memorial Stadium and its surroundings, downtown, or if they have been spent in each other's homes with a televised game and game party– what has made them special are those I have spent the day with. And, of course, it doesn't hurt if Nebraska wins the game.

Mary Jane Nielsen

Chapter Eleven

Game Day: A Day Unto Itself

Big Red Cake

½ cup shortening
1-1/2 cups sugar
2 eggs
2 ounces red food coloring
2-1/2 cups plus 1 tablespoon cake flour
1 teaspoon salt
1 cup buttermilk
2 tablespoon vinegar
1 teaspoon soda

Cream shortening with sugar. Add eggs and beat well. Add food coloring. Sift flour and salt together and add alternately with buttermilk and vanilla. Beat well. Mix vinegar and soda together and blend into batter. Bake 25-30 minutes at 350 degrees in two 8-inch pans.

Frosting

3 tablespoons flour
1 cup milk
1 cup sugar
1 cup butter
1 teaspoon vanilla

Cook flour and milk until thick. Cool. Cream sugar, butter, and vanilla together. Add the cooked ingredients and beat until like whipped cream.

Barbeque Sauce for Smokies or Meatballs

4 c catsup
1 ¼ c brown sugar
2 onions (small) & chopped fine
4 T liquid smoke

Cook on stove until onions are tender. Pour over smokies or meatballs.

Barbecued Spareribs

½ cup catsup
¼ cup vinegar
¼ cup sugar
½ teaspoon salt
½ teaspoon chili powder
½ teaspoon dry mustard
1 medium onion, finely chopped
2 pounds spareribs

Combine ingredients for barbecue sauce. Pour sauce over ribs. Cover and bake at 375 degrees for 45 minutes. Remove cover and brown for 45 minutes.

Mrs. Robert S. Devaney, Lincoln, Nebraska
Nebraska Centennial First Ladies Cookbook

Corn Crib Popcorn Balls

2 Quarts popped popcorn
½ cup molasses
½ cup sugar
1/3 cup water
1 tsp vinegar
1 tbsp butter
¼ tsp baking soda
Red food coloring

Place popcorn in a large bowl and set aside. In a heavy saucepan, combine molasses, sugar, water, vinegar, and butter. Cook over medium heat, do not stir. Heat to soft ball stage or 235 degrees. Add baking soda and stir well. Remove from heat, add food coloring to tint pink. Immediately pour over popcorn, stirring gently with a wooden spoon, coating well. When cool enough to work, quickly shape into 3 inch balls, using oiled gloves. Makes 8 popcorn balls.

Esquire Dip

16 oz cream cheese
1 T garlic powder
½ can beer
1 T horseradish
1-4 drops red food coloring

Combined softened cream cheese, garlic powder, beer and horseradish. Blend well and chill. Serve with pretzels or chips.

Football Soup

1 large can tomato juice
1 pkg dry onion soup
4-5 shakes of Worcestershire sauce
5 Shakes (or less if desired) Tobasco sauce
1 c water
garlic salt or garlic powder
salt and pepper
½ tsp accent

Mix together in a large saucepan: tomato juice, onion soup, Worcestershire, Tabasco, and water. Season with garlic salt, salt, pepper and Accent. Simmer for about 20 minutes or until onion soup is done. If soup is too thick, add more water.

Sammy's Big Red Bloody Mary

Salt the rim of a highball glass with
Lawry's season and celery salt mix
Fill with ice

Shot of Vodka
Fill with Clamato (or tomato) juice
Dash of lemon pepper
Dash or two of Worcestershire
1 tbsp. of any pickle juice
Dash or two of green tobasco sauce
1/8 tsp. horseradish (pure, never creamed)

Garnish with pickle spear,
celery stick or olives
Stir and enjoy

More Game Day Thoughts & Memories

Choosing what Red, White or Black clothing to wear for the day
Checking the weather
Making the trip to downtown
Finding a parking place
Walking to the Stadium
Filling the thermos with coffee
Setting up the tailgate party
Sell-outs
Coaches
Players
Fans
Tailgating
Touchdowns
Traditions!
Rivalries
Devaney Era
Osborne Era
National Championships
Big 8 memories
Big 12 memories
Bowl Games
Taking the bus downtown to the game
Consecutive Sell-outs
Pep band & cheerleaders at Misty's night before the game
Airplane with banners flying overhead
Red Cowboy hats with white N's on them
Red & White Balloons for sale
Solich
Callahan
Home Coming Displays
Marching band through downtown
Red & White Carnations & Mums
with Pipe-cleaner N on them
Red Feather

Pelini Brothers
Rushing the gate
State Fair
Street construction
Smoking banned from stadium
Umbrellas banned from stadium
Crisp fall air
Oscars
Headsets
Hot Dogs
Red wind breakers
Corn cob head
Transistor radios
Big 10
Husker Bob
Hail Varsity!
Husker Power
Red & White Balloons
Painted faces
Barry's
The Russian Inn
Jet flyovers
Grills
Big 8 Days
Tears, Triumphs & Testimonials!
I Need Tickets
I Have Tickets
Scalpers
Cornhusker Hotel (both old and new hotels)
Nebraska Club
University Club
Miller & Paine Tea Room
Kuhl's for breakfast
Chesterfields, Bottomsley & Potts
Parking Lot Tailgaters
Bishop's Gateway – bus to game

Red 9
Denny's
Hilton Hotel
Holiday Inn Downtown
Parking cars
Nebraska has 5 seasons:
Winter, Spring, Summer, Fall & Football
Out of town games
Never schedule your wedding on a game day
Spring Game
Road trips
Stacks of Cups – cup snakes
Touchdown! Touchdown! Touchdown!
Senate Inn Café
Lincoln Hotel
Journal Star
Women in suits, heels & hose
Boy Scouts
Bishop's Cafeteria Gateway
PO Pears
Sidetrack
Sweep Left
Trying not to get drenched with spilled drinks from stadium seating above
Rallies
Homecoming displays
Bonfires
Red Feathers
He's on the 40, the 30, the 20…!
Night Games
Popcorn
Peanuts
Pass-Out check
The guys who paint themselves red
Cheerleaders
Dance Squad
Rock the dock
Grand Manse

Nebraska Bookstore
Tailgaters with big screen TVS
PO Pears Bus – Now Red 9 Bus
Memorial Stadium
Third largest "city" in Nebraska
Game played over speakers in all stores
Stadium seats
Pepsi
Police Tower Guards
Prop plane with advertising sign behind it
Peanuts in the shell
Having to show a student ID with your ticket to get in.
Getting the ID back from who bought your ticket
Stadium Blanket
Tunnel Walk
Helicopter
Val's Before, During and/or after the Game and for home parties
KFOR
KLIN
Radio on in stores during game
Listening to a game at home
Coke – Ice Cold Coke!
No Umbrellas
Big Screen TVs – new and meant something
Cold, rainy game days and hot chocolate
Time Warner Cable/Pay Per View
Pass-out tickets
Husker Bob
The Still
Televised Games & home parties
Buying a program
Oranges tossed on the field for Orange Bowl
Tortillas tossed on the field for Fiesta Bowl
Mad Mike

Der Weinerschlinger
Corn Cob Man
Man, Woman and Child!
Dick Perry
Herbie Husker
Little Red
Half-time show
Visitors
Water boy
Sneaking Peppermint Schnapps into the game to put in hot chocolate
Announcement of special celebrity visitors
Ponchos
The Devaney Show
Californians for Nebraska banner
Alaskans for Nebraska banner
Knothole Section
Sky Boxes
Homecoming King & Queen
The "Wave"
Popcorn
Stadium seats
Ushers
Red Cross
Torn down Goal Post
Frozen toes
Monday Morning Quarterbacks
Where to go after the game?
Paint the Town Red
Corn Crib
Misty's
The Steak House
The Country Club
Tico's
Val's 33rd & Holdrege
Misty's
Runza
KOLN/KGIN Sports
KLKN Sports
ABC
CBS
Froggy 98
Elk's Club
Legionnaire Club
Lee's Chicken's Rooster with "N"
Tony & Luigi's
WOW Sports
KETV Sports
KPTM Sports
Action 3 Sports
Hob Nob
Stooge's
SideTrack
Sweep Left
N-Zone
End Zone
Tropics Lounge
Embassy Suites
The Tom Osborne Show
Bob Devaney's Table at the Legion Club
Bus Tours
Senior's Day
Ramps
Politicians Stickers & fliers
The Knolls
Tam 'O Shanter
Pennants
Half-time favorite haunts
Back 2 Back
Stadium blankets
Purse checks
Lyle Bremser
Haymarket
Mom's Chili after the game
A good night's sleep in Husker Dreamland!

Go Big Red!!!

Cornhusker Blessing

May your game days all be sunny,
With no rain to spoil your fun.
May you always make it to your seat
Before each game's begun.
May the coke man always be near by.
And the restroom lines be short
May you always cheer a play well done
And, in losing, be a "sport".
May the person in the row ahead
Only stand when you arise
May the referees be blessed with brains
And twenty-twenty eyes.
May the Huskers give you much to cheer
And may the scoreboard story tell
That our Big red team has won again
And may the sooners go to ....

Lance Hall